Dr John Taylor, Chartist

Ayrshire Revolutionary

W. Hamish Fraser
Professor Emeritus in History
University of Strathclyde

published by
Ayrshire Archaeological and Natural History Society
Ayr, 2006
www.aanhs.org.uk
printed by
The Cromwell Press, Trowbridge, Wiltshire

Copyright © 2006 by W. Hamish Fraser
All rights reserved. No part of this publication may be reproduced, stored
in a retrieval system, or transmitted, in any form or by any means without
the prior written permission of the publisher, nor be otherwise circulated in
any form of binding or cover other than that in which it is published and
without a similar condition being imposed on the subsequent purchaser.

designed and typeset by David McClure

ISBN 0 9542253 5 X

Until his recent retirement Hamish Fraser was Professor of Modern History at the University of Strathclyde. Among his publications are *The Coming of the Mass Market, Conflict and Class: Scottish Workers 1700-1838,* and *A History of British Trade Unionism 1700-1998.* He has also edited books on both the history of Glasgow and the history of Aberdeen.

For Helen

Contents

Illustrations

Acknowledgements

As ever, thanks are due to many archivists and librarians who have been of assistance in this project. In particular there were the librarians and archivists of the Andersonian Library, University of Strathclyde, the Mitchell Library, Glasgow, the Carnegie Library, Ayr, the National Library of Scotland, the National Archives of Scotland, the Royal College of Surgeons Edinburgh, the British Library, the National Archives at Kew, Newcastle-upon-Tyne City Library, Manchester Central Library, Birmingham City Library, University of Durham Library, Cumbria Record Office, and Tyne and Wear Archives. Many individuals have provided information, listened to tales of John Taylor or answered email queries. Among these were Mr Bernard Aspinwall, Professor Sian Reynolds, Mrs Dorothy Thompson, Dr Joan Allen and Dr Malcolm Chase. Particular thanks are due to Professor Owen Ashton who read an earlier draft and offered much useful advice. I am especially grateful to Rob Close who suggested this biography to me and who has been the source of a fund of valuable information on Ayrshire.

Illus. 1: The statue of Dr John Taylor in Wallacetown cemetery.
(*photo* **Rob Close)**

Chapter One:
'Every inch a man and a gentleman'

16 October 1858, a day of civic celebration associated with the laying of the foundation stone for the new Kyle Union poor house in Ayr, ended with a march to the new cemetery on the edge of the working-class district of Wallacetown. It was a Masonic procession led by the Deputy Grand Master, Sir James Fergusson of Kilkerran and by representatives of the mother lodge of Scottish masonry, Kilwinning. At the cemetery a Mr Finlayson, the Royal Worshipful Master of the Defensive Band Lodge of Edinburgh, unveiled a 7½ foot high statue, of their Masonic brother, Dr John Taylor, upon a marble pedestal 13¼ feet in height. Finlayson, who recalled having seen Taylor in Glasgow, was careful to say that Taylor's political opinions might differ from those of many in the crowd, but declared that he was 'every inch a man and a gentleman'. 'Few men,' he went on, 'possessed a more open heart, or displayed more generosity of character'.[1] The unveiling was the result of many years of effort by groups of Taylor's admirers in Kilmarnock, Ayr and elsewhere. The bearded figure of the statue, with long hair, wears a cutaway frock coat and waistcoat and sports a large bow tie. A dramatic cloak and boots complete the striking effect. The caption on the pedestal reads,

TO

JOHN TAYLOR, ESQ.,

OF BLACKHOUSE, M.D.,

BORN AT NEWARK CASTLE,

AYRSHIRE, 16TH SEP., 1805,

DIED AT LARNE, IRELAND,

4TH DEC., 1842.

HE CONTESTED THE AYR BURGHS

IN 1832, AND AGAIN IN 1834,

ON RADICAL PRINCIPLES;

AND REPRESENTED PAISLEY, ETC,

AT THE CHARTIST CONVENTION

IN 1839.

THIS STATUE

WAS ERECTED BY

PUBLIC SUBSCRIPTION,

IN COMMEMORATION OF HIS

VIRTUES AS A MAN, AND HIS
SERVICES AS A REFORMER.
PROFESSIONALLY, HE WAS ALIKE
THE POOR MAN'S GENEROUS FRIEND AND
PHYSICIAN; POLITICALLY, HE WAS THE
ELOQUENT AND UNFLINCHING
ADVOCATE OF THE
PEOPLE'S CAUSE,
FREELY SACRIFICIING HEALTH,
MEANS, SOCIAL STATUS, AND EVEN
PERSONAL LIBERTY, TO THE
ADVANCEMENT OF MEASURES
THEN CONSIDERED EXTREME,
BUT NOW ACKNOWLEDGED
TO BE ESSENTIAL TO THE
WELL-BEING OF THE STATE.
Requiescat in pace

There is also a verse attributed to Taylor but in fact from a poem, 'Angel Voices', sent to him, shortly before his death, by a young woman living in Edinburgh.[2]

The Dead are here, the blessed, faithful dead.
Whose earthly graves your bitter tears are steeping.
Whose souls, by us through the dark valley led.
Their Saviour holds in His eternal keeping.
Too much ye mourn that yonder heavy sod
Doth hide the lovely from your aching sight.
To little do ye feel that, sown by God.
They yet shall blossom in His bowers of light.

That any Chartist should have a statue is something of a surprise. Studies of memorials suggest that they are either created right away after the death of the person honoured, or in 20-30 year cycles after the death, when groups battle over the collective memory. The 1850s did bring something of what the *Times* called a 'monument mania' and moves by reformers to build monuments to Feargus O'Connor, the best-known of the Chartist leaders, began immediately after his death in 1855. The largest of these was unveiled in Nottingham's Arboretum in August 1859.[3] That one should have been raised to Taylor in Ayr ten months before, sixteen years after Taylor's death and a mere ten years after there was talk of possible revolution in Britain as in the rest of Europe makes it even more surprising.

That it should be to someone who not so long before that had been regarded as among the most dangerous and notorious advocates of physical force as probably the only way to achieve the People's Charter, and who, even in recent works on Chartism, is described as 'a violent demagogue' and 'a hardcore revolutionary' is astonishing.[4] It would seem to indicate that there was an admiration and affection for Taylor in his native Ayrshire which had stood the test of time and which had survived the considerable vilification he had suffered during his life-time.

The biographical information on Taylor is thin and patchy. While Taylor appears in all accounts of Chartism the details on his role are generally slight. Some of what information there is about him was pulled together by Dr Alex Wilson in a lecture to the Society in 1949 and that lecture has been largely the basis of brief entries in biographical dictionaries and in comments on him in various histories of Chartism.[5] A full biographical study is not really possible, given the paucity of material, but the aim of this publication is to expand on the existing knowledge of his career and to try to assess Taylor's contribution to the Chartist movement. It draws largely on scattered references in the Chartist and non-Chartist press, and on the few items in various archives.

What emerges is a complex figure who, even his fiercest critics admit, had an immense charm. Even those who disagreed with some of the sentiments he expressed and disapproved of his drinking and laxity with money seem to have succumbed to that charm. Like a number of the Chartist leaders he presented a flamboyant appearance, with cloaks and unusual hats, open-necked shirts or large, bright cravats. It was a very effective way of drawing crowds at mass meetings and generally catching public attention. In many ways he was the classic 'gentleman leader' or 'hero-politician', which was such a feature of the Chartist movement: exotic, very different from the audience which he was addressing, but, at the same time identifying with them and emphasising his devotion to them and the sacrifices which he had made on their behalf.[6] But, Taylor's Bohemian style pre-dated his Chartist days and seems to have reflected his personality. He was always an outsider. He separated himself from his family and his class by throwing himself into radical causes, but even in these causes he was something of a loner often going against the prevailing grain.

What emerges also is a picture of a widely-read, highly literate man, with a flair for poetry and an oratorical skill in addressing mass meetings that few in the Chartist movement could surpass. There is little doubt about the strength of his commitment to the cause of working-class political rights. He traversed the country, he experienced imprisonment, he sacrificed his always delicate health for the cause in which he believed and, as is evident from the memorial, there were those in Ayrshire who recognised what he had done and appreciated a remarkable man, a 'friend of the people'.[7]

Chapter Two:

'Eyebrow dark and eye of fire'

Illus. 2: Drawing of Newark Castle from *Christian Lyrics.*
(Carnegie Library, Ayr)

John Taylor was born on 16 September 1805 in Newark Castle, then a fairly typical Scottish tower house on the edge of Ayr, where presumably his parents were renting accommodation.[8]   His mother was Annabella Fullarton, daughter of General John Fullarton of Skeldon, who had married Captain John Taylor of Blackhouse in September 1802.[9]   In adulthood, many people commented on John Taylor's swarthy looks.   One paper described his complexion as like that of an Indian Chief, while another identified it as like a Turk. It was through his mother that he inherited these looks since, like many Indian army people in the eighteenth century, the then Colonel John Fullarton had married an Indian, Shanie Chanim of Sindela.[10]   On the other side, the Taylors were relative newcomers to Ayrshire. The family fortune had been made by his grandfather, also John

Taylor, who had trained as a lawyer in Edinburgh. He had become agent for many of the creditors of the notorious York Buildings Company. This company had acquired a number of the estates in Scotland forfeited by Jacobites after the rising of 1715 and the revenues from the estates were used to fund life annuities. The Company's many escapades into various, often dubious, speculative ventures had left a trail of creditors, and 'a thick and palpable darkness had long been gathering over the whole affairs of the company'.[11] But little could be done as long as the annuitants were still alive. However, as these died off, Taylor was able to sell off some of the estates and recover money for the creditors. The recovery of the money continued throughout the 1780s and Taylor got as much as 15 per cent of what was recovered as his commission and payment for his services.[12]

Taylor was one of a group of Edinburgh businessmen who took over Newton colliery in Ayr in 1786, just at a time when industrialisation in Ayr was beginning to take off. It was this Ayr Coal Company which bought the Blackhouse estate in 1787.[13] Taylor senior died in Edinburgh in January 1810 and soon after his death a pamphlet was circulated by a fellow Edinburgh lawyer, Archibald Swinton, accusing him of having embezzled £139,000 of creditors' money over the previous decades. Swinton produced the pamphlet to encourage creditors to take action against Taylor's estate. Taylor's three sons, John, William, and George, took the matter to court and the case rumbled on for a year or more. John, the eldest son, who had had a military career, inherited the estate of Blackhouse in his father's will but because of the legal complications it seems to have been some time before the family was able to take possession. Financial difficulties and uncertainties surrounded the family from the start.

The young John Taylor attended Ayr Academy for a year or two until the age of eight or nine, when he received private tuition from Rev. Dr John Stirling, the minister of Craigie. In his early teens he was sent to Bath, where he was tutored by a John Hall. His removal to Bath may have coincided with the death of his mother and his father's remarriage. At the age of sixteen he became an apprentice to an Edinburgh surgeon, Alexander Gillespie, and received his licence from the Royal College of Surgeons in Edinburgh in May 1825.[14] From the age of 17 he had interest from a substantial heritable bond of £12,500 from his father, to provide him with a small income. His father, however, died on 23 April 1823 and Taylor inherited the Blackhouse estate, but it was an inheritance weighed down by debt, largely incurred by the company John Taylor and Sons of which Taylor *père* had been a partner. The rents were almost immediately sequestered on behalf of the creditors.[15] Shares in various collieries were sold at the end of 1827 and the land and fishings of Blackhouse were sold for £42,000 in November 1828.[16] The debts amounted to more than £46,000, and when the creditors were paid off eventually in January 1830, those with unsecured money owed to them received a mere 1/6d in the £.[17]

At some point after 1825 John Taylor went to France for further medical training.[18] He had, apparently, become politically aware in about 1823 at the age of eighteen, presumably as a result of his experiences in the closes of Edinburgh's old town, and he claimed to have spent his twenty-first birthday in a French prison.[19] In 1827 and 1828 he was still in Paris, a student at the hospitals of La Salpêtrière and L'Hotel Dieu.[20] We know almost nothing about Taylor's time in Paris other than the fact of his imprisonment, but, for any young person these years of one's early twenties are formative ones and his sojourn in France undoubtedly shaped many of his later attitudes. It was a time when there were numberless conspiracies and protests against the restored Bourbon monarchy in France. One historian has talked of 'an epidemic of conspiracy'.[21] The *Charbonnerie*, off-shoot of the Italian nationalist *carbonari*, had been involved in a series of secret meetings and plots against the Bourbons. It was a secret organisation, organised on the lines of Freemasonry and its activities attracted a wide range of young people, especially students of law and medicine, with radical views. The arrival on the throne in 1824 of Charles X, even more reactionary than his brother Louis XVIII, and determined to undo what remained of the revolutionary innovations, increased the tension. Taylor would inevitably have been influenced by the ferment of agitation and ideas swirling around his milieu in Paris. With his Masonic links he might even have made contact with the ultra-radical Société des Amis de la Vérité, which followed the Scottish Masonic rite and which 'became a sort of permanent seminar for the boldest discussions of political and philosophical issues'.[22] These experiences would have confirmed him in the republicanism which was to be a consistent belief until the end of his life. As an historian of Revolutionary Paris has explained, there was more to republicanism than merely an alternative to monarchy. The ideal republic was to be a place of virtue with a strict code of both public and private morality. Republicanism stressed manliness, physical courage and physical strength. The heroes were the heroes of the Great Revolution, Robespierre, Marat, St. Just and others, men of action and men of rhetoric, with a deliberate theatricality in their role. These were men who embraced sacrifice and suffering.[23] All of these were features which, from time to time, Taylor was to seek to emulate.

It is impossible to know how seriously he was involved in revolutionary activities in France. It has not been possible to identify a specific protest in September 1826 which might have lead to his arrest, but there was no shortage of causes of protest in these years. He later talked of belonging to a society to keep an eye on the growth of Jesuit influence. The Jesuits were blamed for most of the attempts to restore clerical control over academic activities in these years. He claimed that the Jesuits at this time had removed bodies from the hospitals and left them around in order to exaggerate the number of murders in the city to strengthen their case for the establishment of a gendarmerie.[24]

He is also likely to have been influenced by the romanticism which, later than in many other countries, swept France in the 1820s, apparent in the paintings of Delacroix and in the poetry of the young Victor Hugo. As is clear from his library, Scott and Byron were among his enthusiasms while in France. The Romantic Age was preoccupied with heroes, solitary figures who were superior to the common herd, men who were dissatisfied with life and hostile to the changes that industrialisation was bringing about. In Byron's work the hero was often an aristocratic rebel who supported radicalism against his class, what has been called 'the noble outlaw'.[25] In France he would have come across renewed admiration for the heroes of the Revolution such as Robespierre. The hero was fiery, passionate and a heroic figure who could influence his followers by his charisma, his determination and his sheer physical courage. The hero was romantic in appearance. Scott's Marmion had a thick moustache and coal-black curly hair, an 'eyebrow dark, and eye of fire'. Byron's Corsair too had a 'dark eyebrow' through which 'shades a glance of fire', 'sable curls in wild profusion' and features that 'more than marks the crowd of vulgar men'. Byron had died at Missolonghi in 1824 while fighting for Greek independence and the Byronic hero was firmly embedded in the popular imagination as 'Byromania' swept Europe. Taylor was probably already developing his Byronic style by the time he left France.

Although it may be that his arrest involved little more than getting caught up in a student protest it provided Taylor at a later date with useful 'revolutionary' credentials. Indeed, he was to claim that he had assisted in the July 1830 revolution which dethroned Charles X and it may be that he did go back to France briefly in July 1830.[26] To complete the image, he seems to have signed on as a naval surgeon in a merchant ship or in one of the ships heading for Greece where the war of independence against the Turks continued. By some accounts he spent an inheritance of as much as £30,000 to fit out a ship to help in the Greek War of Liberation against the Turks. The source of the story seems to have been Thomas Frost in his *Recollections* published in 1880. According to Frost,

Taylor had some years previously inherited a fortune of thirty thousand pounds, the greater part of which he expended in the promotion of revolutionary enterprises, first abroad and afterwards at home. During the Greek struggle for independence, he purchased and equipped, at his own expense, a small vessel, with which he joined the insurgents. He was afterwards concerned in a conspiracy of the French Republicans, and ordered to leave France in forty-eight hours. He was described as a vain, impetuous young man, wearing his long black hair parted down the centre, a fashion very generally adopted by advanced reformers a few years later.[27]

The story was repeated by Max Beer, *A History of British Socialism*, and the source of his story seems to be a reference in an article published in 1873 reputedly based on a 'Private letter from a member of the Chartist Convention':

Dr John Taylor, some years before the Chartist agitation, had inherited a fortune of £30,000 and a valuable mercantile concern. In the next few years he squandered away the one and ruined the other. He was inordinately vain and used to imitate Lord Byron. He spent the last remains of his fortune in the purchase of a small armed vessel with which he joined the Greeks. From Greece he got to France, and was there mixed up with the conspiracy for which the two Beaumonts were tried. He was ordered to leave France in 48 hours.[28]

But there is reason to doubt the veracity of the story. In all the many studies of the Philhellenes there is no mention of such a ship or of such sums of money being donated, or, indeed, of Taylor. Such a contribution surely would have attracted widespread attention since the various Greek committees were always desperate for money. Also, Taylor did not have access to that kind of money. There was no huge inheritance. Significantly, the profile of him in about 1836 in *The Liberator*, a Glasgow Radical weekly on which he worked and eventually owned, makes no mention of his Greek exploits. On the other hand, when he was nominated in Newcastle upon Tyne as their delegate to the Chartist Convention in 1839, the proposer talked of his connection with liberty in Greece.[29] Half a century later his friend, George Julian Harney, noted that he had been involved in the struggle for Greek independence but added 'I neither vouch for nor deny this story'.[30]

Chapter Three:

'An extremely clever but wayward young man'

Taylor was back in Ayr in 1830 and describing himself as a surgeon, based in Cathcart Street, where he was living with his step-mother. He was well connected in the area. His mother's brother, William Fullarton, was Provost on four occasions and his father's brothers, George and William, were involved in various business enterprises in the county. Although described as a surgeon, he does not seem to have practised in the town for long. Certainly he did not participate with the other physicians and surgeons in the town at the beginning of 1832 in looking at measures to deal with the expected cholera epidemic. On the other hand, his experience as a doctor in France, at sea and in Ayr must have made him aware of the dreadful social conditions in which many had to live and begun the process of radicalising his political views. Unlike some of the other doctors who got involved in Chartism, like the Newton-Stewart born Peter McDouall, and James Scholefield, Taylor never got involved in the selling of patent medicines.[31]

He seems to have been facing some financial difficulties by the middle of 1832. The business of Messrs Taylor and Mitchell, surgeons and chemists, was in the hands of trustees and Taylor's library was up for sale. It consisted of a thousand volumes in both French and English. These included rare works such as those of Scott and Byron published by Galignani in Paris, novels by Washington Irving, Bulwer, Cooper and Disraeli; poems by Crabbe, Southey, Wordsworth, Burns, Pope and Dryden and, again Byron. His affairs were still under trust in 1833 and he was working at the Ayr Chemical Company, a family firm, that had operated in Newton on Ayr from about 1815.

He begins to appear on the public scene as the movement for parliamentary reform began to gain momentum in the autumn of 1831. In 'an eloquent and feeling address', he seconded a motion by a fellow surgeon to urge the King to stand firm for the Whig Parliamentary Reform Bill after the House of Lords had thrown it out: 'Shall a handful of self-interested Lords and Bishops be permitted to withhold the boon?'[32] When the Reform Bill eventually passed, amid much excitement in August 1832 he took a leading part in the celebrations. In the procession he marched at the head of the Squaremen, (carpenters) one of the Incorporated Trades of Ayr, and claimed, enigmatically or perhaps just jokingly, that he was partly entitled to do so 'having served an apprenticeship to the business'. He spoke to the crowd just after the magistrates and called for cheers for the Whig members for the town and the county, Thomas Francis Kennedy of Dunure and James Oswald of Auchincruive. He also chaired the dinner laid on especially for the working-class reformers. On that occasion he toasted only Oswald, whom he claimed to have known since childhood, but made no mention of Kennedy.[33]

With the Reform Act on the statute book, a general election was expected soon to test out the new semi-democratic electorate. The constituency of Western Burghs linked the towns of Ayr, Irvine, Inveraray, Campbeltown and Oban. T.F. Kennedy, who had been Whig Member for Ayr since 1818 and one of the authors of the Scottish Reform Bill, called a meeting of electors at the end of September and here, and afterwards in the press, Taylor made his objections to him known. He asserted that Kennedy, who was now in the Government as a Lord of the Treasury, needed to explain his 'somewhat ambiguous' conduct as a reforming MP. Kennedy had recently indicated that he had no enthusiasm for the introduction of vote by ballot, despite admitting that under the existing system there was occasionally the use of undue influence by landlords on their tenants. Kennedy had also been critical of the East India Company, declaring that the governing of India should not be left in the hands of commercial company. Taylor, with his family links to India, declared himself totally opposed to the Government taking over. The East India Company, he claimed, consisted of people who knew the laws, religions, languages and institutions of India. To hand more power and patronage to the British Crown would bring 'the utmost danger to our own freedom'. Like most radicals at this time, Taylor saw the greatest threats to liberty coming from excessive power in the hands of the executive.

The third issue that Taylor raised was reform of the notoriously corrupt government of Scottish burghs, reform of which Kennedy claimed to support, but over which he now seemed less than enthusiastic. The main bone of contention, however, were the Corn Laws. Kennedy had talked of the need to proceed with care before any reform of the laws was introduced lest it destroy the farming interest, and he had advocated a fixed duty on imported corn rather than a fluctuating one tied to the price of grain. To Taylor these were the opinions of a thorough-going Tory, 'expressed in all the cant language, and with all the ambiguity of which that class are so eminently masters'.

Taylor went on to declare his own support for triennial parliaments and for the extension, albeit still limited extension, of the franchise,

to every independent householder, whose intellect and education fit
him for the right use of it. I do not mean that talent and education
which enable him to make successful bets at Doncaster, or return
flushed with gain from the gambling house – I mean that talent and
education which enables him to maintain an honourable character
and status in society, and fit him for consideration of his country's
interests.[34]

He was also clearly incensed that a Whig clique, led by his 'esteemed
uncle', ex-Provost Fullarton, had determined to back Kennedy without even
asking for his views on any of the issues.

Within weeks Taylor had decided to come forward as a candidate of
Liberal principles, 'a determined and uncompromising Radical', 'an
unflinching advocate of the people's rights', committed to 'the greatest
possible good to the greatest number'. His election address reiterated the
points made in his earlier speech and letter with some added issues, such as
commitment to the separation of church and state, to the end of sinecures
and unmerited pensions, to freedom of slaves and to a general reduction in
government expenditure. He was accused by the Whigs of being a Tory in
disguise and his actions clearly caused much bitterness within his extended
family. He told the crowd gathered at the hustings in the middle of
December that 'my acquaintances, with whom I used to associate, have
stood aloof, and my very relations have ranked themselves on the side of
my rivals', while the vilest calumnies had been thrown at him. These
included the rumour that he had been thrown in jail, presumably for debt.[35]

Interestingly, at the hustings in Ayr, where the non-electors gathered,
it was Kennedy, not Taylor, who won the show of hands, but Taylor
received strong backing from Irvine Political Union. In Irvine, it was
claimed that more than once he had been 'honoured by a seat on the
shoulders of the people. ... borne in triumph, in a boat, preceded by music,
flags, &c.'[36] A poll was called for and Kennedy was returned by a
substantial majority, with Taylor winning a respectable 164 votes to
Kennedy's 375 and the Tory, James Cruikshank's 33. More than half
Taylor's votes (87) came from Irvine, where his Uncle William had
extensive business interests. Ayr gave him 41, Campbeltown 33 and Oban
three. From the handful of voters in Inveraray he received none. To Taylor,
Kennedy's victory was a victory for the old closed town councils, who
continued to control local politics.[37]

Undeterred, Taylor now turned his hand to journalism. He may have
first edited a new journal that appeared in Ayr and Kilmarnock at the end of
1831, *The Western Journal*. The publishers were James Donnan and Robert

Nelson, the latter a bookseller in Kilmarnock. It was not a particularly political affair, but a miscellany of satirical and literary pieces, typical of many little magazines at this time.[38] However, in January 1833 he floated his own venture, the *Ayrshire Reformer and Kilmarnock Gazette*. It was printed in Kilmarnock, by James Paterson, a publisher of radical pamphlets and papers at the Ayrshire Radical Press.[39] In the second issue of 22 February 1833 he denounced Kennedy:

> We shall be merciful to this man, because those who do not know us may suppose that we are actuated by feelings of private animosity; we denounced him openly however, to his teeth, on public grounds long ago. We accused him openly of private peculation as a road trustee, telling him personally that we intended to attack him, and requesting the honour of his company to the feast. We opposed him with all our energy, forcing him to acknowledge, and to bend to people as men, whom his niggardly pride, sanctioned and approved by the Town Council of Ayr, (The most infamously venal and ignorant one, by the by, which ever existed in Scotland or anywhere else,) had made him look upon as slaves. We denounce him now again as an enemy to the country; nor shall we cease to do so, till we have seen him disgorge some of the public money which has already slipped over his greedy throat, or give an unquestionable vote in the people's favour, and that is not likely to happen for a little while. He is one of those hollow patriots whom the Whigs bolstered up with all their power ...

He also accused Kennedy of apostasy for his support of the Irish Coercion Act of 1833, which banned public meetings, more or less suspended habeas corpus and imposed martial law in various parts, one of the first signs that the new, reformed Parliament would have little time for popular radical movements. Kennedy sued Taylor, Paterson, the printer, Robert Nelson and Alexander Hutchison, booksellers and stationers in Kilmarnock, for £1000, claiming that the piece had 'traduced his character and endeavoured to bring him into general odium and contempt'.

Taylor seems to have ignored the summons to appear, although the solicitor-general, Henry Cockburn, may have seen him personally in May. Since he was bankrupt, he claimed that he lacked the means to defend himself in court. In June, Taylor signed a letter of apology to Kennedy, but this was returned and the signatures of all the defendants asked for. On 10 September he wrote to Kennedy accusing him of 'ungentlemanly, insulting and tyrannical' conduct and challenging him to a duel. Kennedy immediately handed the letter to the authorities, and Taylor and his second,

James Macalester of Kennox, were summoned before Sheriff Bell. He was not charged with having broken the peace by sending the challenge, since that was a criminal offence which would have come before the High Court of Justiciary, but the summons was to prevent his committing a breach of the peace in the future. On the 12th Taylor and Macalester were each bound over to keep the peace for two years, under a caution of one hundred pounds. Failure to find the necessary caution would result in imprisonment for a period of up to two months. Taylor was unable to find the money and was duly jailed. After ten days, Francis Jeffrey, the Whig Lord Advocate, and a friend and colleague of Kennedy, intervened, since the possibility of criminal proceedings had been raised and a warrant had been issued to convey Taylor, Macalester and Kennedy in custody to Edinburgh. Clearly anxious to avoid the scandal of a government minister being involved in such a matter, Jeffrey wrote to Taylor and asked that he and Kennedy should 'jointly pledge your words of honour before a Magistrate not to have any hostile meeting'. Complaining that the Sheriff's requirement to keep the peace for two years was too all embracing, Taylor, none the less, agreed to pledge himself not to break the peace in connection with Kennedy or anyone else connected with the current issue. Having made the required pledge before the Sheriff-substitute and the Procurator-Fiscal, Taylor expected to be released, but he was now asked to sign a bond, to keep the peace. He refused and, as a result, was told that he would not be liberated. He now asked that his earlier declaration should be withdrawn and that the warrant of the High Court should be put into force, and he penned a legal protest against his treatment. He also wrote again to Jeffrey. But, late in the afternoon of 25 September he was released on the instructions of the Procurator-Fiscal. He immediately rushed into print and issued a twenty-page pamphlet spelling out the details of his confinement and release and accusing the authorities of acting both illegally and unfairly. It ran to two editions and, in the telling, in time became transformed into 'one of the most heart-stirring essays on the liberty of the British subject'.[40]   In December the Court of Session ruled against Taylor and Paterson on the issue of damages, since no defence had been given in. £300 for Kennedy's expenses were added to the £1000 damages.[41]11

It is not clear whether the paper had survived until this time, but the damages certainly would have destroyed it.[42]   The strain of the affair was also clearly telling on Taylor. According to the explanation offered in *The Liberator* 'ill health, produced by over-exertion, compelled him to retire to the country'.[43]   Nevertheless, he continued to take up a number of local causes.   For example, he blocked an attempt to hand over the Burns' monument in Alloway Kirk, which had been erected by public subscription, to the landowner who owned the surrounding land. He organised public meetings of protest. He also involved himself in the battles over a new water supply for the town, objecting to the proposed cost of carrying water from Carrick Hill, and continuing to attack the Town Council for its lack of openness and accountability.[44]

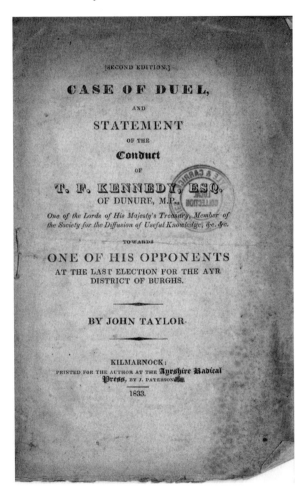

Illus. 3: Taylor's pamphlet on his dispute with Kennedy – 'one of the most heart-stirring essays on the liberty of the British subject.' (Carnegie Library, Ayr)

Nor were his activities confined to Ayr. He must have been active speaking to working people throughout the county, because in October 1833 he was presented with a plate and with a blue Kilmarnock bonnet by the 'operatives of Kilmarnock'. The money had been collected in penny subscriptions. It recognised his 'active, unwearied, but patriotic and disinterested exertions in contending, at all times, and in all places and seasons, for the rights and liberties of the people, for [his] public spirit in detecting abuses, things hidden and unseemly, and having the daring to exhibit them forth to the public in all their deformity; and, above all for [his] Radical principles'.[45] According to the autobiographical reminiscences of his erstwhile collaborator, James Paterson, written forty years later, Kilmarnock 'was kept in a state of excitement by the frequent appearance of Dr Taylor, an extremely clever, but wayward young man'.[46]

Kennedy of Dunure, who himself was facing some financial difficulties, resigned in January 1834 and Taylor immediately offered himself once again as a candidate, 'a determined and uncompromising Radical... "the greatest possible good of the greatest number," being my motto'. His position was that of any middle-class radical. He identified abolition of the Corn Laws and abolition of timber duties as his two priorities. He also called for the separation of Church and state, 'a union, at once unscriptural, impolitic and tyrannical'. He would insist on 'Retrenchment and Reform' and the end of sinecures and unmerited pensions, and he was convinced that vote by ballot, short Parliaments and great extension of the franchise were necessary.[47] For this, he received support from the carpet weavers of James Templeton's factory in Ayr who persuaded their employer to back him as a fellow manufacturer. This time Taylor won the show of hands at the hustings and had a very respectable 213 votes to Lord James Stuart's 305, the latter having not appeared in the constituency at all. He pushed up his vote in Ayr from 41 to 76 and in Campbeltown from 33 to 52, but his Irvine support declined by 13 votes and his Oban support by 8 votes.

The announcement of the result was followed by extensive rioting in Ayr. The rioting was not indiscriminate and seems to have been aimed at voters whom it was felt ought to have voted for Taylor but had not. The windows of the house of Joseph Boyd of Newton Green disappeared under a hail of stones. He had been a clerk and cashier with the Taylor family's Ayr Coal Company and had been indebted to Taylor's father. The windows of James Gray of Newtonhead followed, for the same reason. Then it was on to the houses of leading Whigs who had brought forward Stuart.[48] In the general election in January 1835 Taylor talked of standing again but decided against it lest the seat fall to the Tories. Surprisingly he actually put forward the nomination of a mildly-reformist Glasgow businessman, Alexander Johnstone, standing in the Whig interest, arguing that 'Burghs should be represented by commercial men and men of business habits; counties by the Aristocracy'.[49] But, when a by-election arose in the county seat six months later, Taylor put himself forward declaring that there should be no truck with 'a set of drivelling Whigs' and scorned the claim that he would split the liberal interest and let the Tories in. He did not, however, canvass or make speeches and he retired from the contest at the nominations' hustings.[50]

With his medical practice abandoned and his publishing enterprise bankrupt, Taylor turned to the family for support and from 1833 until 1836 he ran the Ayr Chemical Company, which was part of the business concerns of the Ayr Colliery Company, which had moved into saltpanning and into soda production after 1815. But both areas were in decline and were probably struggling to survive.[51] He also continued to be active in Ayr life. Like a number of other radical, middle-class figures he interested himself in wider European issues and, in March 1834, he took up the Polish cause, helping to set up a committee to condemn Russian atrocities in Poland.[52] In September 1835, he was on the platform during the visit to Kilmarnock of Daniel O'Connell, the Irish 'Liberator' who was still being feted by radicals, a position that was to change soon afterwards as O'Connell identified himself ever more closely with the Whigs.

At the beginning of 1836 Taylor became president of the Ayr Burns Club and received rapturous applause for the Immortal Memory which he gave at the Burns' supper, at the end of which he read an epic poem of his own composition, which tapped into Ayrshire's powerful perception of its history, with,[53]

LINES TO THE MEMORY OF BURNS

When our lost country faction-torn and prey
To England's thirst of conquest, owned her sway
When noble hearts, that knew not how to bend,
Burst in the proud attempt their chains to rend;
And hardy courage, awed, but not subdued,
In straggling bands a deep revenge pursued.
Which every hour brought some disastrous tale
Of new misfortunes, till each cheek grew pale
With rage or terror; then one hero rose,
And made our rage a terror to our foes.
WALLACE! (what heart is here, so sunk in shame,
As not to beat more proudly at the name?)
Wallace, surrounded by a patriot band
Of Airshire's chosen sons, redeemed the land

And, for this very town, first gave the word
That rescued Scotland from a Tyrant's sword.

Next Carrick's Earl, immortal Bruce stood forth,
To guard our rights, and save the sinking North;
While round him still his faithful kinsman stood,
And shed for Freedom Airshire's noblest blood –
Till Europe's champions quailed beneath his fame,
And victory crowned him 'mid the land's acclaim.

Since then, how many a name in history's page
Has shone conspicuous in a later age;
Spain, Egypt, India claimed their blood – to earth
They left their fame – but Airshire owned their birth.
Thus, while our land for worth and valour shown,
In every clime and every age was known,
'Twas left for ONE to add a nobler fame,
And make our home immortal in his name.
Go seek him not among the proud and great,
The high and haughty ministers of state –
Among the titled magnates of the land,
With all that wealth can purchase at command –
Nor 'mid the minions of a court, whose praise
Were worse than degradation to his lays.

By Doon's green bank, in simple guise arrayed,
As from his daily toil but newly strayed,
Serene and thoughtful – over Nature's face
He looks, and finds in every feature grace;
Soars with the lark to greet the opening day,
And half repeats and half inspires her lay;
Or giving voice to daisies, in the moan,
For their neglect but images his own;
Or makes the houseless mousie still realte
How men and mice an equal end await;
Culls from creation round her flow'rets wild,
And plays with Nature like a sportive child.

Where Air's bright waters gently float along,
There, on its banks is heard her matchless song;
Where Girvan rushes to embrace the main,
Her murmuring tribute answers to his strain;
Each smiling rivulet, – each rocky glen, –

Wakes, at his will, to melody again!
While every lovely picture, once so cold, –
Where song was silent, – where no vow was told, –
Touched by the mighty master's hand, awakes,
And all its sweetness in his numbers breaks;
Till each loved scene, so little marked before,
Becomes a classic spot, forgot no more.

Not one fleet age shall claim him as its own,
Nor his loved country twine his wreath alone;
Through every varied clime, – from pole to pole, –
Far as the winds can waft, or waters roll –
His name shall still be honoured, and each song;
In living language shall his fame prolong.
Successive ages, wondering, shall admire
Those simple strains which now our hearts inspire;
Memory, half dead, beside her sinking flame,
Shall re-illume her altar with his fame;
And, till this lovely world to ruin turns,
Shall make our land immortal to our BURNS!

It is perhaps reasonable to assume that the poem is saying as much about Taylor and his ambitions as it is about Burns.

Dependent as we are on the local press for information on Taylor's activities at this time, one can only guess at his other activities. There can be no doubt, however, that he was giving speeches and lectures throughout the county to working class and radical audiences, activities that went unreported in the local papers. It must have been at this period that he established his reputation in Ayr as 'the poor man's generous friend and physician'.

Chapter Four:

'A lava-like eloquence that set on fire

all combustible matter in his path'

James Burn, a hatter and radical trade unionist in Glasgow, came across Taylor for the first time during the visit of the Liberal Earl of Durham to Glasgow in October 1834, a visit that stimulated a renewed demand for political reform. He is described as of middle height, and many who knew him commented on his large, dark brilliant eyes.[54] He had already adopted an unorthodox garb: 'a sailor's dress, with a sort of brigand hat, and the collar of his shirt turned down in Byron style ... his hair was jet black and hung upon his shoulders in graceful curls, and his eyes were large and black as coal'.[55] It was a style of dress that allowed him to be strikingly different from his audience and so catch attention, with, at the same time, the symbolic sailor's jacket, which linked him to his popular audience. It was a common strategy of the gentleman leader, identifying with the mass of the audience while, at the same time, being clearly marked out as separate. The famous Henry 'Orator' Hunt had his white hat and the Chartist Feargus O'Connor was later to sport a fustian jacket but, as Owen Ashton has said 'never presented himself as ordinary'.[56] On the occasion of the Durham visit Taylor presented an address from the reformers of Ayr.[57]

During 1836 he began to involve himself more in Glasgow activities, although in an address to the electors of Ayr Burghs he indicated that he was ready to stand again for Ayr or for the county against both Whig and Tory. In May, he gave his first address in Glasgow at a dinner for the radical candidate at the 1835 general election, George Mills. He was something of a guest of honour on that occasion, being introduced to the assembled guests by Mills as someone who had made great efforts 'to thwart the mischievous schemes of the aristocracy' and who would soon find a seat in Parliament. Taylor, in his turn, 'renounced all connection with Whigs' and called for the battle to be 'between the Radicals and the Tories'. He also continued generating a heroic narrative, recalling his imprisonment in France on his 21st birthday and his imprisonment in Ayr on his 28th birthday: 'In the maintenance of his principles, he had lost his wealth, his health, and his friends, and he was ready also to lose his life'.[58] He made an immediate impact, being described as the 'crack orator of the evening'.[59]

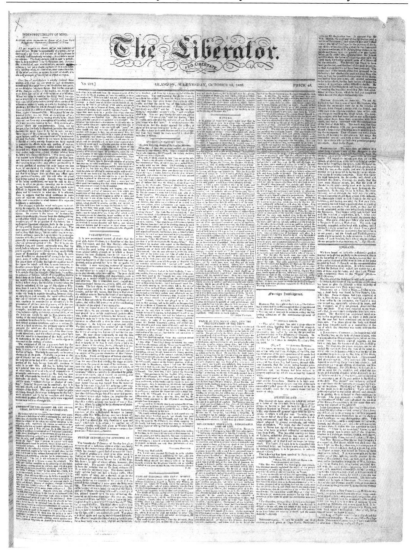

Illus. 4: The front page of *The Liberator,* Wednesday 26 October 1836.
(British Library Newspaper Collection)

In July, he moved to Glasgow to become a joint-editor of *The Liberator*, a radical weekly paper launched at the end of 1832, owned by John Tait, and which was aimed at a working-class readership. It is very likely that he had been contributing material to *The Liberator* over the years, but unfortunately only one copy of that paper survives. A 'large and respectable audience' bade farewell to him in the Theatre in Ayr and 'a number of friends and supporters' gave him a farewell dinner on the following evening.[60]

He probably took a partnership in the enterprise just before Tait's sudden death in October 1836. His appearance continued to cause comment. According to the vitriolic tongue of Peter Mackenzie of the *Reformers' Gazette*, the 'wee laddies' in Ayr had laughed 'at his curly pow and funny looks': 'Some take him for a Jew, others for a Turk, and not a few for a strolling player: he is really so fantastical, whether from nature or design we cannot tell'.[61] He was already sporting a beard, which was very unusual in a public figure at this time. It was another four years before G.H. Muntz, M.P. for Birmingham, became the first parliamentarian of the Victorian period to have a beard. One does wonder whether, in a time when racist attitudes were becoming more open, Taylor was conscious of his Indian ancestry and that this made him an outsider – at least in his own eyes – and inclined him towards radical groups.

Mackenzie, once a Parliamentary reformer himself but now a violent anti-Radical, had been a rival of Tait and *The Liberator* throughout its existence. An article in *The Liberator* in August 1836 was highly critical of Mackenzie and he sued. Before the matter could come to court in November, John Tait died and Taylor was left as owner. Thousands turned out for Tait's funeral at the necropolis, where Taylor – reputedly for the first time in Scotland – delivered a graveside eulogy 'after the manner of the French people'.[62]

At this stage, Taylor was clearly very much part of middle-class reform circles. With William Weir, the editor of the *Glasgow Argus*, and campaigner for repeal of the Corn Laws, he attended meetings of the London Anti-Corn Law Association, and with Weir and William Tait of *Tait's Edinburgh Magazine* became a member of the committee.[63] Indeed, as late as June 1837, Taylor was arguing that repeal of the Corn Laws needed to take precedence over political reform:

> They would leave it (continued Dr Taylor) to the speculating philosopher to talk about Triennial Parliaments, the Vote by Ballot, and education and endowed churches – let them speculate on those as much as they will – but we must have food before we can enjoy any of them (Cheers). Dr Taylor then proceeded to point out the gross and glaring tyranny and oppression of the Corn Laws, pointing out the urgent necessity of first of all giving the people food, before any attempt could be made to instruct them.[64]

Not much came of this particular Anti-Corn Law Association, but it brought Taylor his first contact with another colourful, romantic campaigner, Augustus H. Beaumont, who was also a member of the committee.[65] Taylor was a great admirer of Beaumont, later writing a poem in his memory. Beaumont was another classic romantic, who during his brief life fought no fewer than fifteen duels. The Anti-Corn Law Association also gave Taylor an opportunity to meet some of the middle-class, moderate reforming MPs on the committee, like Joseph Hume, and John Arthur Roebuck.[66]

But Taylor soon became disenchanted when he found that the middle-class leaders showed little interest in the condition of the working class. He had, he declared, no wish to see power transferred from the landed aristocrats to monied ones. He found that the whole aim of the new, wealthy middle class 'was to amass riches for themselves, while the health and happiness of the masses never occupied their thoughts'. They were 'educated to believe that money was the supreme good, the acquisition of it the only noble employment'. At least the landed aristocrat, he argued, had 'some feelings of humanity about him, and some interest in seeing the people about him cheerful and contented'.[67] Meanwhile, all the time, Taylor was developing oratorical skills with what his fellow-Chartist, G.J. Harney called 'a lava-like eloquence that set on fire all combustible matter in his path'.[68] R.C. Gammage, an early historian of the Chartist movement, who knew Taylor, wrote of his oratory,

> He was none of your long-winded prosy speakers, who seem to delight in talking chiefly because they give delight to nobody. Twenty minutes or half an hour was generally the extent of time which his speeches occupy, but during that time the words were poured forth in a clear flowing stream, without a pause that was not correct, in language of the most glowing eloquence, delivered with an air that was truly impressive, his voice though loud, pealed forth tones of the richest music; in short, no orator possessed more completely the happiest combination of natural gifts and artistic power than Dr John Taylor.[69]

Another fellow Chartist, Robert Lowery, claimed that he had 'rarely heard his equal at a speech after a soirée or dinner in a hall, there was such a happy blending of historical and classical allusions, polite literature and poetical sentiment'.[70] Taylor was now well on his way to being one of those gentleman leaders who, according to William Lovett, secretary of the London Working Men's Association, the working class always wanted to lead them.

FEARGUS O'CONNOR, ESQ^R

Illus. 5: Feargus O'Connor by an unknown artist.
(National Portrait Gallery, NPG D5386)

As owner and editor of *The Liberator* Taylor was now established in Glasgow radical circles. In November 1836, he chaired the dinner and presentation to Robert Owen, 'without committing himself to the peculiar views of Mr Owen'. It seems to have been at Taylor's suggestion that Feargus O'Connor visited Scotland in December. O'Connor was rapidly emerging as the most charismatic campaigner for radical political reform, who had been busy trying to form radical associations throughout the North of England. In preparation for the O'Connor visit a Radical Association, with Taylor as president, was formed in Glasgow, which, with Glasgow's ever-growing self-regard, took the title *Scottish* Radical Association. It laid down a programme of universal suffrage, annual parliaments, the ballot and a voluntary church. At the inaugural public meeting, with Taylor in the chair, Alexander Hedderwick and James Turner of Thrushgrove, two veteran reform campaigners, pressed that the target initially should only be household suffrage, but were hugely outvoted. Others talked about the need to accept reform gradually, but the Owenite socialist, Alexander Campbell, in a powerful speech, declared 'that they had been taking instalments too long, and they now wanted their rights'.

The fact that the issue of a voluntary church was on the agenda reflected the extent to which church issues were intruding on the Scottish political scene. Glasgow was aglow with evangelical fervour, so much that someone referred to it in these years as 'Gospel city'. Besides the recurring issue of patronage, there had been, in recent months, bitter protest against proposals for state funding for an Established Church extension programme. An attempt by the editor of the *Weavers' Journal*, William Thomson, to get the meeting to avoid 'mixing up of religious matters with their political movements' failed.[71]

Although Monday 12 December was an evening of lashing rain, O'Connor's entry into the city from Port Eglinton to the Bazaar in the Candleriggs was accompanied by one hundred torch carriers who escorted his carriage. Torchlight meetings were a phenomenon new to Glasgow, and undoubtedly could stir trepidation among the propertied classes. O'Connor's rumbustious style went down well with the predominantly working-class crowd, although it is not clear from the press reports just how great a turn-out his meeting had. Taylor then accompanied him to Edinburgh, where John Fraser, a veteran reformer originally from Johnstone, was also stirring a new reform campaign. Much to the malicious amusement of the *Scotsman*, Taylor was introduced by Fraser as 'the illustrious John Taylor'.[72]

Taylor supported the Whig choice of the local merchant, John Dennistoun, as candidate in another by-election in Glasgow early in 1837, and went out of his way to deny 'assertions being propagated, of operatives being generally desirous of revolution'. But sections of the working class were moving on. The west of Scotland was badly hit by an economic slump in the Spring of 1837. The Owenite, Alexander Campbell, at a working-class meeting on the Green to protest against the desperate unemployment situation linked the condition of an industrious people, who were 'literally starving', with the failures of the political class. Despite the great advances in machinery, hours of labour had not been reduced: 'There are also those who pretend to be the friends of the working classes, and make much noise about the corn laws, in order to produce cheap labour'. To Campbell, society was 'much more radically wrong, than what Radicals generally believe; these *only* cry for universal suffrage, vote by ballot, annual parliaments, no money qualification, and no corn laws', but much more was needed to change the position of the working class.[73] To Campbell, also, with an echo of Taylor's comments, 'money aristocrats' were much worse than 'our landed aristocracy'.[74] It was a sign of a much more class-oriented tone to which Taylor, as self-appointed spokesman for the working class through *The Liberator*, began to respond.

Relations between Radicals and Whigs further soured when Taylor offered himself as a candidate for Glasgow in the general election of July 1837, in the aftermath of Victoria's accession, when a group of Taylor's supporters declared that Lord William Cavendish Bentinck, former governor-general of British India, one of the two sitting Whig members, was not a fit and proper person to represent Glasgow. The radicals published a campaigning song entitled 'Wha's like us!'. It began,

> Again the greedy, gripin' Whigs
> Wad bind the people foot and neck;
> But brawly noo we ken their rigs,
> An' winna at their biddin beck.

After denouncing the 'rusted Lordlin', 'A stranger to you and me', it ended,

> Then here's to sterling TAYLOR JOCK,
> Wha daured consistency to play;
> His head is but a Barber's block
> That wad presume to say him nay.
>
> A reemin' bumper no we'll drink
> Tho' Whig and Tory should gae mad;
> Down wi' the Cleek and auld Bentinck
> An' Toast about that "*Jack's the lad*"!

Whigs and many fellow radicals were highly critical, conscious of the dangers of the 'Liberal' vote being divided and of a Tory creeping in. Taylor, accused of having been paid by the Conservative candidate, Robert Monteith, to split the Whig vote, was howled down at one meeting and, such was the uproar, had to leave the meeting by a back door.[75] A warrant was taken out against Taylor for debt the day before the candidates' nominations had to be submitted. As a result, he could not appear at the hustings and he was jailed for some weeks.[76] A new bitterness of tone began to enter Glasgow politics, between the Whigs and the Radicals. Taylor no longer hid his 'hatred and opposition to the Whigs, whom he considers by far the most dangerous foes to freedom'. Mackenzie's *Reformers' Gazette* scoffed at him with 'A Dirge to the "Illustrious" Dr John Taylor'.[77]

Haste, haste, mighty Radical! Haste to thy rest
Thy political course is run,
Make speedy retreat to retirement's calm breast,
And enjoy the prize thou hast won.

Haste, haste, mighty Radical! Haste to thy rest;
Pause not for a moment to shed
A tear of compassion o'er Liberty's breast
She despises the fool who's misled.

Haste, haste, mighty Radical! Haste to thy rest;
Prolonging the time is in vain;
No party can claim thee; dropt now is thy crest,
And nonedescript now is thy name.[78]

As a result of the writ Taylor, once again, went bankrupt. A large part of his debt was to the printers of *The Liberator*, W. & W. Miller, but, ominously, there was also the colossal sum of £65 (about £3250 in today's money) due in bills to wine merchants. Despite this, Taylor, with some others, managed to launch the *New Liberator*, a four-page broadsheet priced at 4½d, which he printed as well as published and edited from a house at 38 St Andrew's Square in Glasgow.

During the year, Taylor had been an active campaigner throughout the west of Scotland, receiving presentations from many different towns for his efforts. Radical women from Ayr presented him with a gold medal and chain, 'probably the first ever in Scotland presented to any public man' according to *The Operative*, and there was a similar presentation from the women of Cumnock at the end of 1837.[79] No doubt his good looks and his impeccable manners worked their charm on his audiences every bit as much as his radicalism. Sometime during the year also he published a sixpenny pamphlet, *Letters on the Ballot*, arguing the case for the introduction of a secret ballot at elections.[80]

In the summer of 1837 the members of the Association of Operative Cotton Spinners struck work in the West of Scotland. It had for many years been one of the strongest trade unions in Britain. *The Liberator* was not particularly sympathetic to the strike. Taylor believed that trade unions were necessary if working people were to get a fair share, but he saw strikes 'like rebellions in a state' and 'of a highly dangerous tendency', which should only be embarked upon when 'carefully considered, well-matured, and proper arrangements made to ensure success'. He deplored the fact that different trades had got involved in recent years in sectional skirmishes when what was needed was unity across all trades.[81] However, the arrest of the leading officials of the Cotton Spinners' Union in August, after a strike breaker had been shot, and charges of murder laid against them, stirred deep class division in Glasgow and elsewhere.[82] Taylor 'in one of his most brilliant orations in defence of the rights of working men', according to the Newcastle *Northern Liberator*, declared that the arrest of the cotton spinners' committee was 'something deeper than an attempt to get a few men hanged for murder – something that struck at the roots of the rights of working men'.[83] At a meeting in Newcastle of more than 5000 people to hear Feargus O'Connor and Augustus Beaumont, the assembled meeting 'testified their delight by repeated cheers' at Taylor's arrival on the platform, according to the report in his own *New Liberator*.

Now the *New Liberator* adopted a more militant tone suggesting that it was possible that the assassination of the blackleg, Smith, was 'at the request of the masters, in order to enlist against the spinners the sympathy of the public, and to furnish themselves with an excuse for conduct so damning, that it could only escape execration during an excited state of the public mind'.[84] It also set out to re-unite radicals and trade unions behind a demand for universal suffrage. What caused especial bitterness was the slowness to bring the cotton spinners' leaders to trial. Three times the case was postponed at the request of the Crown. In December, the original indictment was abandoned and a completely new fifty-page one, called 'criminal letters', was drawn up, as the authorities scrambled around for evidence to link the unionists with violence against strike breakers that had stretched over two decades.

Taylor was ill during much of November, but at the end of the month he dragged himself from his bed, declaring, 'no man has the right to be ill at such a time', and he was again at a meeting of trade unionists and others to demand an inquiry into the conduct of the public authorities as regards the cotton spinners. It was not about the five cotton spinners, he declared, it was about the tyranny of government, and if the working classes were not stirred from their lethargy they were 'rivetting the chains upon [their] own necks'. He saw the assault on the cotton spinners union as the start of a wider assault on working-class rights. Amid cheers, he talked, with the rhetorical flourish of the romantic hero, of buckling on his sword, alone if necessary, to resist and 'every blow I struck for freedom would soften my path to the grave':

> Our first appeal in favour of the rights of these men now suffering for the rights of labour has been to the laws of our country. Swindled out of justice there, our present purpose is an appeal to parliament; should that fail, and possibly it may, our last resort is an appeal to arms. I confess that I have little hopes from the good will of parliament, but much may be expected from their fears.[85]

Most of the business elite in the city no doubt was contented to see the leaders of the cotton spinners under lock and key, but the *Glasgow Argus* reserved judgement on their culpability until after the trial. As the voice of the Liberal section of the business community it was also pressing hard for at least some reform, with the leader column in each issue having the masthead, 'Vote by Ballot'. The Reformers of 1832 were very conscious of the extent to which they were losing support and they blamed much of it on the pressures that could be exerted on voters by landlords. Looking at the elections since 1832 they could see the number of Conservatives being returned going up at each election, and shrinking majorities for reformers. County seats had reverted firmly into the hands of the landed class, there was relatively little success in small burghs, and, even in the cities, Tory minorities were becoming larger.

November 1837 also saw the publication in Leeds of O'Connor's *Northern Star*, which was to prove to be the most significant organ of the Chartism and whose foundation, James Epstein suggests, should be taken as the start of the Chartist movement.[86] Its timing was fortuitous, since it came after Lord John Russell's 'finality' declaration, that there would be no further parliamentary reform, had left the radicals in turmoil. It covered the background to the cotton spinners' trial and published extensive reports on it from the Edinburgh-based radical bookseller and newsagent, John Fraser. The arrest and trial of the cotton spinners also marked for many the final parting of the ways from the Irish leader Daniel O'Connell, once seen as a potential leader for a reform movement, but who was now firmly aligned with the Whig government. He had violently condemned trade unionism and called for a parliamentary inquiry into the activities of unions. The Edinburgh Radical Association sent a critical letter to the London Working Men's Association deploring their invitation to O'Connell, 'whilst he is the very soul and pillar of those Whigs who would give us UNIVERSAL BANISHMENT in preference'.[87]

At the end of 1837 a group of Birmingham reformers associated with the Radical banker, Thomas Attwood, and the Birmingham Political Union, that had been one of the most effective pressure groups for Parliamentary reform in 1831-32, issued an address calling for a national petition to demand universal suffrage and the ballot. It called universal suffrage 'a rightful inheritance'; demanded the ballot 'for protection', and sought triennial parliaments, as in days when there was 'old and wise rule'.[88] The address was taken up with vigour by Glasgow reformers. A meeting called by the middle-class Reform Association in Glasgow, which was dominated by wealthy businessmen, proposed a petition for the ballot and a vague call for an unspecified extension of the suffrage. The moderate Reform Association called for suffrage extension, with Alexander Campbell, James Moir, George Ross and John Taylor all speaking for nothing less than universal suffrage. Taylor asked why the working class would consider petitioning just for an unspecified extension of the franchise. The reason the Whigs were losing support was that the working class had now decided that there was nothing to be got from the Whigs. Taylor, seconded by a newcomer, a successful wholesale shoemaker, George Ross, argued that an extension of the franchise had to take priority over the ballot and that it had to be universal suffrage.[89] William Weir, of the *Argus*, declared his support for universal suffrage 'in the abstract', but argued that existing circumstances had to be taken into account and something less accepted.[90]

At the end of the year, as the trial of the spinners drew near, O'Connor, Augustus Beaumont, who could match Taylor in Byronic extravagance, and who owned the Newcastle paper, *The Northern Liberator*,[91] and Joseph Rayner Stephens, fiery Stalybridge clergyman and campaigner against the new English Poor Law, arrived in Scotland, probably at Taylor's invitation. Taylor had met them in Newcastle where they addressed a meeting of North of England Working Men's Association on Christmas Day. Taylor moved the resolution in favour of universal suffrage and 'declared his anxiety to settle the question by the sword',

> The time for physical force had arrived. … It was high time to lay down the spade and take up the sword. … He knew he was talking what was called treason, he had been in the habit of doing so for some time. … He should not object to stand in the dock of the Cotton Spinners – not that he was much enamoured of martyrdom but it would give such an impulse to his principles that he should not object to sacrifice himself.[92]

This notion that he was prepared to sacrifice himself to the cause was one to which he was to return ever more frequently.

He then accompanied his fellow radicals to Glasgow for a meeting on New Year's Day in the Bazaar. Beaumont tapped into his own and into

Scottish interest in Canada, denouncing a policy that had driven Canadians to rebellion and 'has set the blazing torch to the cottage, and burned alive, indiscriminately, men, women and children', and calling for a volunteer force of 500 men to support the rebels. While declaring that they all abhorred the idea of civil war, but 'if we cannot obtain freedom without it, then welcome the barricades'.[93] Taylor seconded Beaumont's resolution but only briefly, suffering apparently from the effects of over exertion.[94] He was followed by Stephens who enlarged on the theme of class war at home:

> To support the unholy, devil-formed conspiracy of the capitalist against the labourer, is our whole land covered over with barracks filled with armed soldiers, who, it is expected will murder their brothers, who are trying to live by their labour ... we shall wrap in one awful sheet of devouring flame, which no army can resist, the manufactories of the cotton tyrants, and the palaces of those who raised them by rapine and murder, and founded them upon the wretchedness of the millions whom God – our God – Scotland's God – created to be happy.[95]

In Edinburgh the meeting on Tuesday 2 January was also, purportedly, on the issue of Canada, but Stephens, amid much uproar, again diverted on to the issue of the trial of the spinners, due to begin the following day. The division of society into 'two unequal parties, viz. the rich oppressor and the poor oppressed' was improper; a large standing army was 'not consistent with a right state of matters' and now there were plans for a rural police, 'an army of spies – with which better to keep the country in subjection'. Taylor rounded the meeting off linking it all to the issue of universal suffrage.[96] However, the aftermath of the meeting was reputedly a night of heavy drinking, and sometime in the early hours Taylor and friends sallied forth and began ringing doorbells in the fashionable New Town of Edinburgh! He, with one of his companions, was arrested and charged with being 'drunk and disorderly'. They were released on condition that they appeared the following day before the police magistrate. Taylor failed to appear, although his friend did and was duly fined a guinea. A warrant was issued for Taylor's arrest. The story seems to have been first reported by the *Glasgow Chronicle*, but was then taken up by the *Scotsman* and made much of by Peter Mackenzie in the *Reformers' Gazette*. As a result of this affair, he missed attending the trial of the cotton spinners.[97]

Perhaps to avoid arrest under the warrant, Taylor travelled south long before the trial had ended on the 11th. He went first to Leeds on the 8th where he joined O'Connor, Augustus Beaumont, and Sharman Crawford, another Irish politician who had taken up the campaign for political reform, at a Radical meeting. Here Beaumont talked of hanging the party leaders and 'knocking out the tax gatherer's brains' while Taylor, in contrast, made a plea for middle-class support. He regretted the break up of earlier class unity.

> Before the Reform Bill was proposed you were a firm and united body bound in the adamantine links of interest and friendship; you pressed forward with one accord, and victory crowned your efforts, now however, how different is the scene? Society is divided into casts [sic]; envy and jealousy have taken the place of affection and esteem and the bonds of equality and fellowship rent asunder, since one man has power to tyrannise, while the other is under the necessity of submitting.

But the suffrage was the natural right of everyone and needed also to be protected by the ballot.[98] At a dinner in the evening, however, his talk was wilder, declaring that 'the time for physical force had arrived; … it was high time to lay down the spade and take up the sword'.[99]

The tensions between different parts of the emerging movement began to appear. In London, William Lovett's Working Men's Association had been critical of the tone of Beaumont, Stephens and O'Connor and for this they were denounced by Taylor as 'sham Radicals … who sneak to the Whig Reform Associations'.[100] The London Working Men's Association was blamed by O'Connor, in a letter to John Fraser, for the government's decision to appoint a Select Committee to investigate combinations of working men and which it was feared would lead to repeal of the 1825 Combination Law which allowed trade unions to exist.[101] Early in February Taylor, 'the handsome republican' is reported lecturing in Dumfries, speaking 'more treason than was ever strung together or heard in the town of Dumfries'. He defended the Canadian rebels, using a phrase that was to become familiar in his rhetoric. If it were in his power he would 'draw his sword on their behalf':

> He would answer the resolutions of Lord J. Russell with the rock of a rifle and the sweep of the sabre, and hoped his countrymen at home would try by some means of redressing their grievances.

He also condemned the apprenticeship system which had been imposed to replace slavery in the West Indies, claiming that the condition of blacks was worse than before and 'that the day was not far distant when they would cease to be connected with the Crown of England'. Despite his constant need for money, the money raised at these lectures went to Dumfries' charities.[102] In April he was reported to be staying in Stranraer, perhaps on his way to or from Ireland, where his sister lived, and lecturing to well-attended meetings on political economy and on the 'Political Rights of Women'.[103]

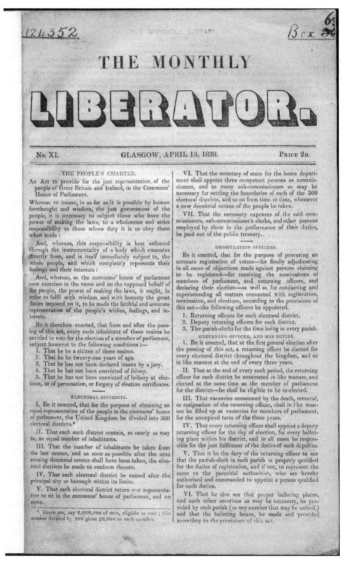

Illus. 6: *The Monthly Liberator,* **13 April 1839.**
(Mitchell Library, Glasgow)

The Birmingham reformers decided to launch their national campaign for a petition calling for an extension of the franchise with a tour of Scotland, starting in Glasgow. The aim was to generate a mass movement that through the constitutional means of petitions and meetings would prove irresistible by government. The London Working Men's Association sent its own delegation to join them and to press the six points of reform, which quickly became the 'People's Charter'. The Glasgow rally of 21 May 1838 was the first to present both the Charter and the petition and its model was followed by many other towns. The Birmingham Reformers were greeted by an archway of evergreens at Tollcross and the words 'Moral force will emancipate the world', so it is no surprise that Taylor was not asked to speak at the Glasgow meeting, although, a few days later, he welcomed the delegates from Birmingham on behalf of the radical reformers of Ayr at a meeting in Kilmarnock. He had clearly been ill and the press commented on his much altered appearance, a change 'not for the better'. In his speech he referred to his poor state of health and, indeed, 'held out no hope of his again being able to address his Kilmarnock friends'.[104]

Despite the middle-class nature of the Birmingham Political Union and the careful moderation of the language of the radical leaders, the demand for universal suffrage, in the face of overt opposition from a Whig such as Russell, was a step too far for many of the middle class, who were unwilling to see all property qualification for the vote disappear. Peter Mackenzie, the former secretary of the Glasgow Political Union, took the view that it was 'extremely unwise even to moot the question of universal suffrage' at present.[105] By July 1838, however, more than 70,000 in Glasgow had signed the national petition.

John Taylor, gradually recovering, became more raucously militant. His *New Liberator* had had to be abandoned as a weekly in April, but the now *Monthly Liberator*, run by his associate, the radical bookseller, John Cumming, led with calls for physical force, 'the only weapon now left to the productive classes, the last argument of freemen'. 'Aristides' (the *nom de plume* used by Taylor) enthused over the plan for a general strike, over the whole country, on a single day and noted how the former leaders of the Reform Bill had stood aloof from the May demonstration, 'because for once you acted upon principle, and expressed your determination in no ambiguous language, which would allow them a loop-hole for escape, when the time arrived for cheating you again'. Now the need was for 'a revolution brought about by the display, and, if necessary, the application of physical force, because it must be evident to every one that, as the country cannot starve, they must strike open the doors of the bonded warehouses, and if the military attempt to prevent them, strike up the bayonets, or strike down the men'.[106] He returned to the theme in an address 'To the people of England' in the *Northern Star*.

> Men may have different opinions on this point, – for my own part I most unhesitatingly state, that I believe it will only be obtained by the sword, and that the sooner you begin to prepare yourselves for the struggle by arming yourselves, the more enabled you will be to take advantage of arms when the time for action arrives. ... I am a revolutionist also ... I never yet heard of a revolution effected by moral force – the only revolution I ever heard of was the passing of the Reform Bill. Now, in the first place, I maintain it was carried by physical force, and, in the second place, I dare any man to say that it has been productive of anything but misery for the nation.[107]

The choice of a sixth century BC Greek philosopher as a pseudonym was perhaps significant. Aristides the Just, as he was known, had been an unbending upholder of justice and liberty who believed in the importance of all citizens serving for the public good. He prided himself on an impartiality to friends and enemies alike and refused to gain from public office. At the same time, he was not a great believer in democracy, but rather in aristocratic rule.

Taylor's reappearance led to renewed attacks on him by Peter Mackenzie, denouncing him as a Tory Radical and as someone 'whose character can be vouched for at the Glasgow and Edinburgh police offices'. Significantly the Glasgow Radical Association distanced themselves from him, saying he was not their leader and 'is only acting on his own responsibility – not being even a member of the Committee'.[108] It is highly likely that Taylor had been borrowing money from some of his fellow radicals, some of whom may have invested in the *New Liberator* and lost their money. According to the Newcastle Chartist, Robert Lowery, who disapproved of Taylor's violent language, for some time he had been living off friends:

> he had outlived all sense of shame and honesty, and would without hesitation make use of any money he could get into his possession, and laugh the parties in the face, telling them he had been obliged to use it, but was to receive such and such sums by-and-bye, when he would be able to accommodate them.[109]

There would also have been disapproval of his drinking among the predominantly teetotal leadership of Glasgow Chartism. O'Connor claimed that he had frequently to defend him against such critics in Scotland.[110]

At Taylor's invitation, Feargus O'Connor undertook a west of Scotland tour in July and Taylor accompanied him at many of his meetings. In Kilbarchan, in Renfrewshire, O'Connor ridiculed the Scots for not taking advantage of the fact that Scotland did not have a property qualification for MPs in order to return a working man to Parliament: 'You Scotch are an aristocratic crew, and would sooner bow to a tyrant than advance one of yourselves'. But his message was clear, 'first get universal suffrage and don't be putting the cart continually before the horse, then when the reins are firmly in your hands you will be able to guide the State in peace and safety'.[111] In the Glasgow Bazaar, O'Connor was praised by Thomas Gillespie, the secretary of the Universal Suffrage Association, for the role he had played on behalf of the cotton spinners, but in his speech he asserted, 'Let the people obtain Universal suffrage and there will be little need for trade unions'.[112] O'Connor was undoubtedly gaining popularity in Scotland and Taylor saw him as someone who could connect the activities in Scotland with what was going on in England.

Victoria's coronation in that same month of July 1838 was marked by a celebration in the Black Boy Tavern in Glasgow's Gallowgate, 'to show their contempt of illuminations, and all the degraded foolery of coronations'. Taylor, 'that stern Republican', as he was described, was the guest of honour and he spoke, once again, against attempts any longer to maintain good relations with Whigs. The meeting linked a number of different strands of radicalism, but the key figures in it were relatively unknown.[113] Thomas Gillespie, a sub-editor on *The Liberator* and active campaigner on behalf of the imprisoned cotton spinners, praised O'Connor, while James Walker 'eulogised the beloved and benevolent Robert Owen'. The bookseller, William Love, called for a national system of education to get it out of the hands of the established clergy, who are interested in 'keeping the people in ignorance'. Others toasted the cotton spinners, 'our Canadian brethren', the memory of John Tait and Augustus Beaumont, while Taylor denounced John Arthur Roebuck and other middle-class parliamentary reformers and trimmers and spoke of 'the folly of attempting to conciliate men who would not be conciliated'. He also toasted 'the Female Reformers of Scotland'.[114] These had made their presence known in a letter 'To the Women of Scotland' in O'Connor's *Northern Star*, in the previous week. Reputedly from a woman weaver in Glasgow, it claimed that the women of Scotland were taking up the cause of Radicalism: 'It is the right of every woman to have a vote in the legislation of her country, and doubly more so now that we have got a woman (the Queen) at the head of the government'.[115]

After a hectic two years in Glasgow, Taylor had cut his ties with middle-class radicalism and had become firmly identified with the Chartist cause. His oratory and his writings had provided a powerful stimulus to the emerging movement. At the same time, he was beginning to align himself with the more militant elements within that movement, increasingly ready to use the language of the threat of physical force as part of his rhetorical vocabulary. As a result he found himself distanced from many of the leading figures in Scottish Chartism who were largely committed to the constitutional road to reform. On the other hand, there is plenty evidence that his colourful style and fiery speeches could get a warm response from the rank and file and had made him a favourite of the women.

Chapter Five:

'To strike down the tyrant

who tramples down the rights of the poor'

During the summer of 1838 there was much activity spreading the message of the Charter to different parts of the country. Working Men's Associations, Radical Associations and Universal Suffrage Associations sprouted everywhere, usually outcrops of previous reform groups. They gathered signatures for the great petition for the People's Charter and plans were announced for the holding of a National Convention in London. Taylor, who was now back in Ayr, was approached by Chartists there and in Cumnock to offer himself as a delegate. He responded with enthusiasm, claiming that he had long supported the idea of a convention and, indeed, later suggesting that he had been the first to propose such a body. He asserted that calling together a convention would bring to an end 'the eternal recriminations bandied at each other through the press'. He was critical of those former reformers who were now 'tampering' with the Whigs'. 'They have become "Moderatists" with expediency as their motto; their next step will be unblushing Whiggery'. There was too much public radicalism, he declared, followed by private recanting and there must be no 'attempt to amalgamate with the Whigs'. The Cumnock people agreed to support him as delegate to the first Chartist National Convention in 1839 against his friend and associate John McCrae, a local schoolmaster. But, at the county meeting in Kilmarnock Cattle Market on 10 November, it was Bailie Hugh Craig, a draper from Kilmarnock, and long-time reformer, who won the nomination against Taylor and McCrae.[116]

In November 1838, Taylor came up with a proposal to form what he called Dhurna Societies, as a way of exerting pressure on government. In India there was a custom of a creditor shaming his debtor into paying up by sitting 'dhurna' outside the debtor's house and refusing to eat until the debt was paid. It had recently been carried into a political protest when hundred of thousands in Benares had demonstrated against the imposition of a house tax by the East India Company, by sitting 'dhurna' outside the city. By refusing to purchase highly-taxed items such as alcohol, tobacco and tea, and even articles of luxury which were taxed, like horses, carriages and dogs, Taylor argued, people could force the government into submission in a relatively short time. There was also the example of the American colonists, who in protest against the stamp duty had boycotted imported items. Taylor proposed boycott as a tactic to be adopted by the Convention, arguing that 'men who would not sacrifice their luxuries from principle, would not fight from principle'.[117]   Robert Lowery had been putting forward similar ideas in Newcastle.[118]   Taylor's scheme was publicised in John Fraser's *True Scotsman*, as a leader headed 'Taxation, Misgovernment, Means of Redress' rather than as a signed article by Taylor, perhaps reflecting Fraser's distaste for Taylor's violent language on other occasions.

> Suppose that of these [eleven million of the working classes] only 2,000,000 were impressed by a conviction of the truth of the views here promulgated, and really desirous of promoting Reform, both social, and political and moral, and that concentrating their efforts, they were, upon a given day, to commence sitting 'dhurna' upon Government, by abstaining from the use of exciseable articles before named, and were to continue the same for six months only, they would be at the end of that time 4,000,000 richer themselves, and Government would be 2,000,000 in arrears.[119]

By the middle of December he had an Ayr Dhurna Society formed, whose members committed themselves to abstain from those exciseable items for the next six months, starting on 20 December. Their buying power would also be used to exert pressure on the shopkeeping class through exclusive dealing only with shopkeepers who were pledged to support universal suffrage. The scheme also had the attraction of involving women in the campaign; Taylor was always enthusiastic about such involvement. The Ayr Society also planned to approach the Tee-total Abstinence Society (a movement which was growing in strength in these years) to see if they could be persuaded to join forces in the campaign. It seemed to Taylor that his plan could help unite reformers by allaying 'the fears of the timid, without in the least dampening the courage of the more ardent'.[120]

On 4 December, he was nominated by the Sandholes district of the Renfrewshire Political Union as a candidate for the national convention. In his reply to the invitation he reiterated his view that the threat of physical force was necessary, just as it had been in 1832, to force change: 'Nothing but fear will make our tyrants relax their grasp'.[121] He was not necessarily talking about actual violence when he mentioned physical force.   His argument was that the threat of violence from a united people was all that would be necessary. On that same day that he received the invitation from Renfrewshire, the issue of moral force versus physical force blew up as a result of the increasingly violent language and appeals to arms coming from Joseph Rayner Stephens and others in the north of England, who were campaigning against the New Poor Law. At a meeting of a hastily-called

Chartist conference in Edinburgh on 4-5 December, attended by only some 20 delegates, resolutions were carried unequivocally denouncing

> in the strongest terms, any appeals to physical force, any exhortations to purchase arms, being fully persuaded such appeals tend to diminish the vast influence of moral power—to draw the people away from its use—to rouse and keep alive the lowest and worst feelings of their nature, to tempt them—smarting, as they are, under a sense of manifold wrongs and sufferings—to make unlawful attacks on persons and property, disgust and alienate the best friends of human freedom, and to bring disgrace on the sacred cause.[122]

On the following day, at an open meeting on Edinburgh's Calton Hill, John Fraser, his associate Abram Duncan, and the radical minister of Paisley Abbey Church, Rev Patrick Brewster put forward similar resolutions condemning any appeal to the use of physical force. John Mitchell of Aberdeen seconded the main resolution, as instructed by the Aberdeen Working Men's Association, declaring 'let the banner of universal suffrage be unstained with one drop of human blood'.[123] Brewster was particularly hostile to the factory reformer, Richard Oastler and to Stephens, because of the ferocity of their language, while at the same time quite prepared himself to use their language of 'white slavery'. The Whigs, he argued, had to be won over: 'Bad as the Whigs are, they are better than the Tories'; 'As they had compelled the Whigs to do with black slaves, so also they must now compel them to set free white slaves'. O'Connor, he still believed, 'with all his delinquencies, was an honest man'. The others, however, had to be swept aside. He rejected the argument that in all circumstances resistance to those in power was wrong. But he went on,

> So terrible, however, are the effects of a national convulsion and so ruinous to the prosperity and happiness of a people, that resistance, even to a manifestly unjust and tyrannical government, can only be warranted, where redress is otherwise impracticable, and where the means of resistance, are such, as to give a reasonable hope of successful issue. It is well for us in this favoured land, that our free constitutional system supplies the means of correcting every abuse, without having recourse to any other measures than such as itself recognises and warrants.[124]

In a sermon at this time, he argued that revolutions in the past in Britain and France had not led to the transfer of power to the people but had resulted in the 'restoration of a government equally interested in maintaining inherited and exclusive privilege'. Indeed, it gave governments the opportunity to augment their own power.[125] These Calton Hill resolutions were to cause a permanent split in the movement. Should violence be ruled out from the outset or should the position be 'peaceably if we can, forcibly if we must'?

Taylor reacted to these resolutions by taking up the case for physical force with renewed vigour. He had been invited to come forward as one of the delegates for the Convention from Newcastle. It is not entirely clear why they should have thought of Taylor. He had been in Newcastle a year before and his speeches on behalf of the cotton spinners had been well-reported in the *Northern Liberator*, but his profile during the preceding months had been low. On the other hand, there were former Ayrshire miners in the rapidly expanding Northumberland coal fields who had worked in the Taylor family mines. Perhaps significantly, it was the miners' leader, Thomas Hepburn, president of an earlier Newcastle Working Men's Association, who seconded his nomination. In Newcastle he found a place where the language was more like his own. In October, the Northern Political Union had declared that 'it is the sacred and imperative duty of every individual Englishmen to be in possession of such defensive arms as are guaranteed him by law'.[126] Taylor appeared before his Newcastle audience on Christmas Day 1838, distinctively clad in 'green hunting-coat, white breeches, top-boots, broad-brim, and had on a red flannel shirt with open neck – man-of-war's fashion'.[127] Here again was the 'gentleman's' rig-out coupled with the orator's hat and the working man's shirt, important symbols to an audience most of whom would have been unable to hear the speeches. He told them,

> He had fought with the pen till the apathy of the people had obliged him to lay it down; he had fought on the hustings until his own apathy had forced him to retire; but he would part with his sabre only with his life, and when all else had forgotten him, his own hand would write his epitaph upon a tyrant's brow, in characters of blood with a pen of steel.[128]

He claimed to have been an advocate of radicalism in Scotland for fifteen years and denounced those who had criticised Stephens and O'Connor on the Calton Hill as 'a set of villians' and as 'mushroom politicians who had sprung up yesterday'. He reserved particular wrath for the Rev Patrick Brewster, 'the meddling priest'. He found himself enthusiastically endorsed as one of the three Newcastle delegates to the National Convention.[129]

At a meeting soon after on Glasgow Green, his language became even more colourful: 'if any coward tell me, that in no circumstances am I to fight for my country's freedom, I will "bite off my tongue and spit it in the tyrant's face" '. However, he quickly came under attack in the pages of the Newcastle paper, the *Northern Liberator*, and the criticisms were copied in the Scottish radical press. He was accused of inconsistency and of having condemned physical force when he was in Scotland and moral force when he was in Newcastle. In a piece by him in John Fraser's *True Scotsman* on 22 December, advocating Dhurna Societies, he had criticised advocates of physical force 'as designing men, leading the people astray from the only certain means of obtaining their freedom'. Three days later at Newcastle he was denouncing the moral force advocates 'as designing men, who were swerving the people aside from the battle for liberty'.[130] The writer in the *Northern Liberator* urged reformers 'not to place the slightest confidence in him, or any of his few contemptible, and suspected supporters!' He defended himself in a letter from Barrhead in which he denied that he had ever been critical of O'Connor and Stephens, but arguing that his exclusive Dhurna scheme should be tried 'before an appeal to arms'.

He blamed the attack on him on personal animosity since he had agreed to take on the editorship of the *Newcastle Operative*, a planned rival to the *Northern Liberator* backed by William Byrne and the Whig-Radical *Gateshead Observer*.[131] Beaumont had recently sold the *Northern Liberator* to the intellectual Morpeth hatter and furrier, Robert Blakey, and to Thomas Doubleday, secretary of the Northern Political Union. Presumably, it was not yet clear what line the paper would take under new management. Taylor may have seen an opportunity for a paper with a more militant line. On the other hand, he may just have been desperate to find a source of income. He had perhaps also caused offence among some locals by getting himself selected as a delegate for Newcastle, although his fellow delegate, G. J. Harney, was also an outsider.[132] The third delegate, Robert Lowery, never liked him, regarding him as having no principles and 'having nothing to lose was prepared to pander to the passion of the hour without heeding the future'.[133] At the end of January Taylor claimed that he had met with the people of the iron-working village of Winlaton, one of the most enthusiastic centres of Chartism in the North-East of England, and they had given him a vote of confidence. He also announced that in future, he would make Newcastle his home.[134] O'Connor, acting as mediator between the rival factions, persuaded the *Northern Liberator* people not to pursue the issue of Taylor's inconsistencies. Taylor seems to have tried to mollify them by saying that he had had to adjust his language for a Scottish audience. A vote of confidence in O'Connor, Stephens and Taylor was accepted.[135]

In Paisley, Brewster failed to persuade the Political Union to adopt the Calton Hill resolutions. The original intention of the moderates was to propose Bailie John Henderson, a radical of 1819, who now owned the *Glasgow Saturday Post and Paisley and Renfrewshire Reformer*, as the member of the Convention. But, probably fearful of being defeated, Henderson withdrew and at a meeting, called at short notice, on 27 December, proposed Brewster. It was the prospect of Taylor being chosen as delegate that seemed to determine Brewster to put himself forward as a candidate instead of Henderson. However, at the nomination meeting in Thornhill on 1 January 1839, Brewster tried to push through moral force resolutions and, when this failed, foolishly marched out of the meeting with his supporters, leaving the field to Taylor. Supporters of Brewster in the Renfrewshire Political Union now tried to overthrow the decision. A further meeting was called with the aim of unseating Taylor. The secretary of Renfrewshire Political Union claimed that Taylor had told him that the members of the Political Union were bound to support him 'not only with their money, but with their persons and their lives' and, on another occasion, that he would shoot any man who tried to arrest him for membership of the Convention. Yet another questioned Taylor's commitment to abstinence since he had been seen drinking in Paisley. Suggestions that he had merely been tasting, and that what he took was for medicinal reasons, were met with much laughter.[136] At an adjourned meeting of the Union Taylor refused to recognise John Henderson, owner of the *Paisley and Renfrewshire Reformer*, as chairman, claiming that he was biased and that his paper had made false accusations against Taylor. He tried to mollify his critics by emphasising his proposals on Dhurna societies. He even withdrew the term 'villains' to describe the Calton Hill people, but reasserted his resolve that 'should all other means fail, *to carve out justice with the sword'*. In the end, after a meeting lasting seven hours until three o'clock in the morning, the attempt to unseat him was lost and Taylor headed for London as delegate for Renfrewshire, Newcastle, Carlisle, Wigton, Alva and Tillicoultry.[137] The Renfrewshire Union split, with the officials and most of the Council breaking away to form a new Political Union.

The National Convention met in the British Coffee House in Cockspur Street in London on 4 February 1839 before moving to Dr Johnson's Tavern in Bolt Court, off Fleet Street. Despite his earlier language, Taylor's position in the early days at the National Convention tended to be on the side of caution. As Brian Harrison has pointed out, he, like the Irish firebrand, Bronterre O'Brien, tended to be more moderate inside the Convention than outside.[138] He was a member, with William Lovett, whom he came to admire, of the Committee for Extending Political Information which decided to send out political missionaries to canvass signatures for the petition and money. Together with Bronterre O'Brien, he was also given the task of trying to rouse London and the Home Counties, where there was concern that the lack of response was harming the cause. When Hugh Craig, representing Ayrshire, proposed that the Convention discuss 'ulterior measures', in other words what action would be taken should the petition be rejected, Taylor spoke against it, saying that such a discussion should wait until after a deputation to members of Parliament had reported and until there had been more discussion with constituents. He did not support the criticisms of the Convention coming from George Julian Harney and the wilder spirits among the London democrats. At the same time, there were occasional outbursts. He warned against the government's use of spies and agent provocateurs. When Harney and his group from the East London Democratic Association, took to wearing red caps and *tricoleur* sashes and to demand that the Convention take immediate steps to prepare for the seizure of power by physical force, Taylor took a lead in condemning such posturing, suggesting that attempts to 'introduce matters at once criminal and dangerous ... looked like a conspiracy to destroy the Convention'. He did not, however, support the calls for their expulsion of Harney and his associates.[139] Taylor declared that he was there 'not to agitate, but to deliberate and to act ... if necessary' and he deplored their tendency to behave as a clique and to present themselves 'as something wiser and better than the rest of the Convention'.[140] None the less he played an active part in trying to stir interest among the London working class, participating in numerous meetings. He also gave assistance to Bronterre O'Brien with his paper *The Operative* and, on at least one occasion, acted as editor.[141]

When at meetings around the Convention there was talk, by some, of arming, tension within the Convention increased. Taylor's language became more extreme. He urged resistance to the impending introduction of police forces into rural areas:

> You may submit to it in the South of England – the men of the North, I tell you will not. I know the men of Newcastle better. I know the men of Winlaton, of Carlisle, of Sunderland, and Wigton, and before such a scheme can be put in force there, you will hear of many a bloody struggle; and when all else has failed and England is subdued, every valley in Scotland shall be a battlefield, the union with England repealed, and the country one smoking desert ere such force be permitted to exist.[142]

When Alexander Halley, the delegate from Dunfermline, spoke out against any reference to physical force, Taylor asked that this should not be seen as typical of Scottish opinion, 'for his constituents held a very different opinion; many of them were armed and none would lay them down'.[143] At a meeting in the Crown and Anchor Tavern in March 1839 he declared that,

> He believed that if the people showed a steady and decided front, and were ready for ulterior measures, they would never need to use them. He might be wrong, those in power might be mad enough to place in opposition to the people, the people's liveried servants – the troops. He thought they would not. But if they should be so disposed, he would tell them in language too plain to be misunderstood, that his constituents in the north were in that position that a single spark would set the Kingdom in a blaze.

Amid cries of 'Bravo', he went on,

> The men of Lancashire and Yorkshire and Northumberland were not to be trifled with – and if it should come to a struggle, it would not be the hand of the dandy that would best use the sword – but the black band of his colliers who were accustomed to the pick. If those in power acceded to their wishes, they would not ask them to resign an acre of land of which they had robbed them; nor to give up their titles, their dignities, their courts, or their palaces; nor to abandon the hells of St James's nor the other haunts of vice and pleasure, but merely to restore to the people the right to which they were entitled – not by the Constitution – but by God himself – Universal Suffrage. When all moral means for obtaining the people's rights should fail, he would claim the post of danger, and be the first to sound the tocsin. (bravo, bravo).[144]

The issue of the right to bear arms came to the forefront at the Convention. Reginald J. Richardson in a speech in early April, later published as a pamphlet, argued for the right to possess arms for defence: 'it is their duty to take care that those arms are in constant readiness to oppose foreign aggression or domestic tyranny'.[145] It was an argument that had its roots in the eighteenth century and earlier when, it was argued, that an armed citizenry was necessary for the preservation of constitutional liberty. To many Chartists the right to bear arms was tied to their concept of 'true citizenship'.[146]

Yet, at the same time, Taylor seemed anxious to try to hold the Convention together. When the three delegates from the Birmingham Political Union walked out in protest at the language adopted by many in the Convention, Taylor claimed that he wanted to try to conciliate them and to get them back into the Convention. He was despatched to Birmingham with O'Connor and others to try to maintain Birmingham support for the Convention. There he addressed the Women's Political Union, whose secretary was one Mary Ann Groves. He blamed the *Morning Chronicle* for mis-reporting the speeches made which had driven out the Birmingham men. As so often, his statements were ambiguous.

> Men called him violent. It might be so; but he had never used a violent expression or done a violent action throughout his whole life, save in defence, nor never would he. But if it be violent to strike down the tyrant who tramples down the rights of the poor, then he confessed he was violent. ... The only safety valve of the people was the Convention. They looked to it as their last hope. They would be quiet only so long as the Convention ordered them; but so sure as there was treachery from within, or an attack from without, there would be such a flame raised throughout England, as would be quenched only by oceans of blood.[147]

He had a second debate with Thomas Salt, one of the Birmingham delegates, but by now it was clear that the Birmingham group would not return. His language now became less conciliatory. He jibed at the readiness to accept laws, such as the Poor Law Amendment Act, which, he asserted, the Scots would never have accepted. He claimed that in Scotland people were ready to fight for their political liberties, just as in the past 'they had drawn their swords in defence of their religious liberties', and that any attempt to impose rural police, as was happening in England, 'would set the heather in a blaze, and would leave every field a field of battle'. The passing of the Rural Police Bill, which reminded him of the attempts by Charles X in France to impose authoritarian rule, ought to be 'the signal of rebellion all over the land'.[148]

By 3 April he was presenting himself to a meeting in the Bull Ring as having rescued Birmingham 'from the fangs of a party who are prepared to sacrifice the people the moment that reform came to their own class'.[149] On Easter Monday, he was in Leeds with O'Connor deploring the lack of militant action there. According to a hostile source, Taylor does again seem to have been strapped for cash at this time. He owed a bill of £20 to his hotel in Birmingham and had to get an advance from his Renfrewshire committee.[150]

The original date for presenting the Petition was to have been 6 May, but a government crisis meant that it had to be postponed. The prospect of a possible Tory government aroused fears among the delegates that the authorities would act against them and Taylor supported O'Connor's proposal that the Convention move its meetings from London to

Birmingham. He still argued that it was possible to put an end to the divisions among the Birmingham radicals, but at the same time, he seemed to be suggesting that the members of the Convention would be safer in Birmingham than in London. In London, he said that they 'could not distinguish friends from foes', whereas in Birmingham 'they would be surrounded by a power no Government would attempt to break through'.[151] He proposed that simultaneous meetings should be held throughout the country during Whit week, 20-25 May, and he also strongly supported an address drafted by Bronterre O'Brien, which proposed that people should acquire arms. Taylor declared that the time for that had certainly come, 'whether it was legal or not'.

In early May the Convention met in Birmingham and, at Taylor's suggestion and against the advice of O'Connor and Bronterre O'Brien, it was agreed to issue a manifesto to see if supporters were 'prepared to act up to certain measures'.[152] As the delegates were dispersing the authorities in Birmingham arrested two of the Birmingham delegates to the Convention, Edward Brown and John Fussell. It was a deliberately provocative act by the magistrates since the charges related to speeches made in March. Taylor and O'Brien, who were still in Birmingham, addressed a large crowd in the town's Smithfield. At one point the crowd turned angry when two police informers were identified, but Taylor implored them to avoid violence against the men.

With the Convention adjourned until 1 July, the delegates headed home to sound out their constituents in a series of simultaneous meetings. On Whit Monday, 20 May, Taylor was at a large meeting on Newcastle Town Moor with Harney and Lowery, where he spoke of the advantage of a general strike of colliers, suggesting that if they were to strike work for a month then London would be a ruin.[153] He predicted an impending crisis in government with more radical Whigs being brought in to replace the Prime Minister, Lord Melbourne, and he warned that, at the same time, the government was looking for a pretext to unleash the military on an unarmed populace – 'but he hoped they would be deceived when they counted on an unarmed population'. He also, once again, wrapped himself in the cloak of heroism, saying that he had been warned of the danger of arrest, but 'if there was danger his place was among the people'. Warming to the theme, he talked of a hundred thousand being ready to go to the battlefield for liberty.[154] At the same time he cautioned them about allowing themselves 'to be goaded into acts of violence by paid spies' and optimistically suggested that they were winning, since the politicians were at each other's throats.

At Carlisle, on the following day, he and Harney addressed an enthusiastic demonstration where he again talked of the possibility of the government using troops against the Chartists and defended the right of the people to be armed. He played on his image as a revolutionary.

> I am called a violent man – a revolutionist, with the spirit of a Marat and the heart of a Robespierre; let them call me so; but this I say for these men whom history has so much vilified, that there never were two bolder or braver spirits in any country, at any time.

He also declared himself willing to accept household suffrage, 'as an instalment', as long as it included lodgers. If it was just ratepayers then it would be rejected. Then it was on to Wigton where he was presented with a green silk scarf and then, at the head of about a thousand marched to Aspatria for another meeting. In both places, according to the Tory *Carlisle Journal*, the speeches were more violent than those in Carlisle.[155] On Thursday, he was in Penrith, where the magistrates in panic had called out the yeomanry. On Friday he addressed a meeting in Kendal with a speech of studied moderation, according to the *Star*.

> If Dr Taylor has not brought over the middle classes and the shopkeepers to our side, he has at least deprived them of their prejudices by presenting Radicalism in its true colours, and breaking down the barriers which misrepresentation has created.

Then it was on to the evening mail coach to get to Kersal Moor in Manchester the next day for the great meeting there. Attendances of anything between 30,000 and half a million were claimed at that. Taylor, his voice hoarse, addressed some of his comments to the large number of women in the audience. Again he argued for restraint:

> The first step towards being free is to know that you are slaves; the second is to wish that you were not so; the third is to try to alter it (cheers), and then the game is won (Cheers). Now you and I are very near this stage; and if you give your enemies no handle, by holding your meeting peacefully, legally and calmly, as you are doing now, you will soon be on the winning sides; for the game is winning itself for you.[156]

For his more moderate audience at a Glasgow demonstration the tone stayed soft and he spoke mainly about exclusive dealing, proposing that chalk marks be put on the doors of shopkeepers who were not sympathetic to the Chartists. One of the attractions of targeting shopkeepers, he argued, was that it would involve women in the movement and he had great faith in women: 'If they had been as far advanced everywhere, as in these towns where the women took the lead, he was convinced they would have gained their rights long ago'.[157]   In Paisley he was presented with a Glengarry bonnet complete with three eagle feathers at a huge demonstration at which he, once again, denounced 'the arch-priest and arch-fiend Brewster' for spreading disunion and disturbance.

The first anniversary of the Charter launch was celebrated by a sedate affair in Glasgow Trades' Hall in May, complete with some clergy and reforming editors.   But the main demonstration was organised on the Green, on the evening of 10 June.   It was intended as a working-class affair. The idea was that workers would join in their working clothes when they finished work.   As always, there were striking displays of flags and banners. A red flag with a hand clutching a dagger had the caption, 'O Tyrants will you force us to this'.   A skull and crossbones declared 'Death shall be the tyrant's lot'.   All shades of Chartist opinion were there.   John Collins from the Birmingham Political Union, John Frost, the Welsh magistrate who had recently been removed as a Justice of the Peace by the Home Secretary, Lord John Russell, R.J. Richardson from Manchester, Bronterre O'Brien, Peter Bussey and Laurence Pitkeithly, the Anti-Poor Law and Factory Reform campaigners from Yorkshire, Robert Lowery from Newcastle and Taylor were all there to speak on the Convention's proposals. James Moir, Glasgow delegate to the Convention, chaired the occasion.

Frost spoke of the danger of more arrests of Chartists, which had been happening since April, and talked of seizing some of the leading men in the country 'as hostages for the safety of the Convention'.   Richardson in a speech full of sarcasm, which occasioned much laughter, encouraged them not to pay money into savings banks, since such money would be used 'to buy a musket for the army'.   Taylor, on the other hand, returned to his favourite theme of exclusive dealing: 'if they chalked up the doors on each side of the streets, and marked every shopkeeper who would not assist them to gain their freedom, they would soon bring them to think that the working class were fit for the exercise of the franchise'.   Bussey concurred, claiming that 'the way to a middle class man's head was through his pockets'.

The English delegates proceeded to tour central Scotland giving speeches, and Taylor was at some of their meetings.   At a Paisley meeting he was reputedly nonplussed when after he had ended with a flourish about 'writing liberty with a pen of steel in letters of blood' an old weaver muttered sceptically, 'Aye, aye!   Doctor, ye kill them an' I'll eat them; I'll eat a' ye kill.'[158]

There was growing anxiety among the authorities at the popular excitement.   In early May, an attempt by some of the Kirriemuir manufacturers to reduce wages led to a crowd armed with sickles and scythe blades and bludgeons attacking the house of one of the manufacturers and assaulting the sheriff's house.[159] The military had to be called in from Dundee, using the new Newtyle to Glamis railway. Such was the anxiety that the Home Secretary, Lord John Russell himself, got involved, instructing that whenever any Chartist demonstrations were expected the Sheriff Principal should ensure that the magistrates were clear about their duty to maintain order.[160] The Provost and Council of Forfar were more relaxed about a Chartist meeting planned for 15 June 'unless persons professing extreme anti-popular opinions shall interfere and provoke those who are equally extreme on the other side'.[161] The Solicitor General, on the other hand, had advised 'that it might be better to move the troops, so as to bring them in sight of the populace, till the meeting was over'.[162] At the same time, W.G. Burns, Dundee's delegate to the Convention, was doing nothing to calm things with a disclaimer of any threat to life or property accompanied by the threat 'that if any of the mill spinners were to assist the military at putting down Chartist meetings, the people would be justified in destroying their mills', while Peter Bussey talked of everyone owning a musket for defence.[163]

Throughout June, Taylor undertook a heavy programme of speeches in the west of Scotland, Paisley (four times), Barrhead (three times), Kilbarchan, Johnstone, Elderslie, Renfrew, Eaglesham, Dumbarton, Tillicoultry, Alva, Bonhill, Alexandria, Hamilton and Glasgow, as well as in Newcastle, Carlisle and Wigton in the North of England.

At the end of the month he and other Chartist speakers returned to Glasgow to a meeting in the Bazaar on behalf of the imprisoned cotton spinners, now in the prison hulks at Greenwich. O'Brien pointed to the economic significance of the trial. The jury, he claimed, had consisted of 'farmers, wine merchants, landlords, shopkeepers and others interested in the reduction of the wages of labour, in exchanging their property for the cheapened labour of the artisan'. At the same time, O'Connor rushed north and offered himself at the nomination hustings occasioned by the death of the Glasgow MP, Lord William Bentinck. On a show of hands, O'Connor had a clear majority over the Whig nominee, James Oswald, and at a meeting in the Bazaar was greeted amid cheers as 'the Member for Glasgow'. In the end, he withdrew from the contest proper on the grounds that he had more to do with his time and money.[164]

The Convention re-assembled in the Golden Lion in Aston Street, Birmingham on 1 July. James Moir, the Glasgow delegate, pressed for a return to London 'to be on the spot, to avail itself of any embarrassment in which the Government might be placed', but Taylor backed O'Connor to stay in Birmingham.[165] For some, the packed meetings across the country during the past month had re-energised them, but many of the middle-class delegates failed to return. Taylor was one of those who was reinvigorated and he pressed the Convention to come to a decision on ulterior measures as quickly as possible. He claimed that in his travels he had 'invariably found the people ready and anxiously looking for ulterior measures … and ready to obey the fiat of the Convention without hesitation'. He reported that in Tillicoultry there were rifle clubs practising daily and that many people had rifles. But they lacked bayonets that would be necessary against cavalry. On the other hand, he had no doubt that 'the sacred month was the same as physical revolution' and, therefore, he urged Chartists to put the idea aside for the moment and to concentrate, instead on withdrawing money from the banks, exclusive dealing and 'to use their constitutional principle of arming as soon as possible'.[166] None the less, he proposed that they meet on 13 July, the day after the petition was delivered to parliament, to set a date for the start of the 'sacred month', the general strike.[167] There were fears of the arrest of the delegates and Taylor was defiantly claiming that 'on the day of the arrests, there were 100,000 men ready and prepared to set Birmingham in flames' unless they were restrained by their leaders.[168] The excitement and the hyperbole around the Convention mounted, with mass meetings being held daily at the Nelson monument in the Bull Ring. On 4 July these were provoked into rioting.

Lord John Russell had been concerned for some months about unrest in Birmingham and had doubts about the vigour with which the magistrates were acting. Birmingham had only recently become an independent borough and did not yet have its own police force. As early as May, four police officers from the Metropolitan Police had been sent to organise the special constables. By the end of June the Mayor had requisitioned artillery for use in the town. Additional Metropolitan police were despatched to the city and on 4 July these, armed with cutlasses and batons, immediately charged a meeting in the Bull Ring, a meeting place of reformers since at least 1831. Crowds gathered there to hear speeches and to have radical newspapers read to them. When the police attacked, some of the crowd pulled down the railings of the nearby St Thomas's Church to use as weapons, and drove out the police. The crowd was dissuaded from going further by Taylor and his fellow doctor, Peter McDouall, warning against a 'premature outbreak'. But rioting continued and Taylor helped rescue two policemen who were about to be beaten by the angry crowd. None the less, he, along with eighty others, was arrested. At one in the morning, he was dragged roughly from the back parlour of the Red Lion Hotel in Digbeth by the police and soldiers and brought before the magistrates at 4.30 for an examination that lasted no more than five minutes. As he wrote to his friend, James Arthur, in Carlisle,

> I was chained by the ankle to another, and there were three others in like manner. The policemen bundled us into a carriage along with five others in a carriage before us, and we were escorted by dragoons, riflemen, and London policemen, in glorious array, and the Mayor, aldermen and magistrates mounted behind us with all the pomp and appearance of war.

He was despatched to Warwick gaol, where he was stripped and had his hair cropped. Bail was set at £1000 and it was three days before he was released, after the intervention of the MP for Warwick and with bail put up by O'Connor and a Mr Smith of Birmingham.[169]

Comparisons were immediately made with the Manchester Yeomanry's attack on a reform crowd in the Peterloo 'Massacre' of 1819, with a fellow Scottish Chartist, William Burns, declaring 'If the magistrates Peterloo us, we will Moscow England'.[170] A placard was produced by the Convention condemning the arrest of Taylor and the others as 'another convincing proof of the absence of all justice in England, and clearly shows that there is no security for life, liberty or property until the people have the same control over the laws which they are called upon to obey'.[171] For this the signatories, John Collins and William Lovett, were arrested and eventually sentenced to a year's imprisonment. Yet another riot broke out in the Bull Ring with the shops set alight of people 'who had rendered themselves particularly obnoxious to the people by their recent conduct'.[172] Taylor wrote daily letters from his cell in Warwick Gaol to his various constituencies, describing his treatment, in particular the shaving of his fine head of 'black flowing hair, parted in the middle, and hanging in long curls below his broad shoulders'.[173] One such to Newcastle was quickly turned into a handbill and circulated throughout the North-East. In it, after the account of his arrest and treatment, he wrote,

> Birmingham is quiet; but effective preparations are being made for a renewed struggle at no distant date. The police have behaved most infamously, and mischief will come of it; even the middle classes who pay the police are disgusted. Arm! Arm!! Arm!! At once, quietly and effectively; be ready to defend your homes from the lawless tyranny of the Government. My trial comes on the 25th. I will plead for myself.
> Rumours have reached us of riots in Manchester. Lovett and Collins were arrested last night. It is said that 40 warrants are out against us,

and that we are to be arrested tonight. No matter, be ready, cautious and discriminate till the 13th – when in all probability the day of the sacred month will be fixed. Again I say, arm! arm!!. Send copies to all your friends.[174]

There was particular excitement in Newcastle, with nightly meetings and talk of a general strike among colliers.[175] A letter arrived at the Convention from the secretary of the Newcastle Political Union claiming that as soon as the news of Taylor's arrest came through 25,000 colliers and the town trades went on strike. It proved to be untrue, but it may have been enough to persuade the Convention, on 15 July, to call for a 'national holiday' or 'sacred month'. It was carried by thirteen votes to six, with five abstentions. A week later, however, urged by O'Connor who argued that there was no adequate preparation and 'no proper organization amongst the people', the Convention agreed to pull back and to leave it to the localities to decide what to do.[176] As O'Connor pointed out, 'Dr Taylor over and over again stated that of the numerous meetings that he attended, not one of them was prepared for the Sacred Month'.[177]

Addresses of support for Taylor poured in from his constituents. In Newcastle, meetings of protest and indignation, at the end of July, erupted into a full-scale riot, the 'Battle of the Forth'[178] and, according to T.A. Devyr of the *Northern Liberator,* there were at this time some 60,000 pikes manufactured in and around Newcastle. The Birmingham attack, he claimed, 'exasperated the Democracy all over the country' and many commenced the work of preparation for an uprising.[179] The Vale of Leven took Taylor's arrest as confirmation that 'before the people of this country can achieve their freedom, they must have arms in their hands'. Similar sentiments came from Barrhead, while the radicals of Alva, 'male and female' thanked him for his kindness and his 'condescension in regard to correspondence'.[180]

The petition, with 1,283,000 signatures, ineffectually presented at long last by Thomas Attwood,[181] was duly rejected by the House of Commons on 12 July. Joseph Hume and Robert Wallace of Kelly, were the only two Scottish members who supported Attwood's motion, calling for acceptance of the petition, although Wallace made clear that he favoured only household suffrage. The Convention, back in London, turned again to the discussion of what was now called a national holiday. James Moir argued that whatever happened it had to be simultaneous and nation-wide 'otherwise they might pull down the houses of those opposed to them and sacrifice many lives, and yet not succeed in obtaining their rights'. William Burns, who had in the past been associated with Fraser and Duncan, argued that there was no alternative but to go ahead with it, if they did not want to cover themselves in disgrace. On the other hand, he clearly felt that they were on a hiding to nothing – 'if we went forward we were lost, and if we stood still and retreated, we were lost'. But he asked, if there was a need for 'a bold step', as people had been arguing, in order to avert revolution what was the alternative.[182] It was agreed that a strike should be called for 12 August, but on the 6th, O'Brien and O'Connor issued an address calling off the strike.

Chapter Six:

'One of the most dangerous characters in the movement'

Taylor came to trial 2 August, bedecked in a pink shirt, green neckerchief and the blue sailor's jacket, which he regularly sported. His case was pushed back for another five days and then no evidence was offered and he was discharged. Why no further action was taken against him is not at all clear, since by this time hundreds of Chartists were being arrested and sentenced for language much more moderate than that of Taylor. According to Peter Mackenzie's paper in Glasgow, he was discharged because 'crown counsel looked upon him as fitter for Bedlam than anything else', which hardly seems an adequate explanation. Perhaps, the authorities felt that there was little chance of a conviction if Taylor could argue that he had actually saved the lives of policemen. It may be that he was showing signs of a recurrence of his ill-health and this deterred them.[183] Certainly, Taylor seems to have been badly shaken by his arrest and treatment. Arrests were becoming widespread and the hefty twelve-month sentences on the mild-mannered Lovett and Collins were undoubtedly intimidating. His friend, Bronterre O'Brien, was arrested in London, and Taylor accompanied him to Bow Street. At a meeting in London on 12 August, chaired by O'Connor, where Chartists marched from Farringdon Street to Kennington Common, and demanded the release of Lovett and Collins and the remission of sentences on the Birmingham rioters who had been sentenced to death, Taylor was one of the main speakers. He claimed that the state of his health meant that he could not be as effective as usual, but none the less, it did not curb his invective. He declared that if London were not prepared to do something, he would rely on the men of the North.

> There were two ways of applying physical force. Stopping the supplies was one. The other the meeting could guess. The combined movement alone could effect the first, but a chance part might do the other. The combined movement had been thrown back by the vacillation of some and the treachery of others, but the combustible materials remained. His hand would light them. It would not be long wanting. (Cheers). If they keep London in hot water by their peaceable meetings, he would take very good care that it was kept boiling in the North.

After that he seems to have headed to Cumberland where he began to hint at dramatic events to come. The authorities in Carlisle were already anxious about Chartist activities in the area. The clerk to the magistrates was in touch with his opposite number in Newcastle, since he was of the belief that any real outbreak would take place simultaneously in Cumberland and in Northumberland. The Chartists, he claimed in early August, were meeting secretly and it was proving very difficult to get information on what was planned. The 'national holiday' had been declared for 12 August and on that day many weavers came out on strike in Carlisle, Dalston, Wigton and elsewhere in Cumberland. But other workers, on the whole, failed to join them. Taylor, while he was in London, kept in touch by letter, 'each successive letter distinguished from its forerunner by the increased violence of the language', according to the Carlisle town clerk. Reputedly, Taylor was saying he would arrive and put himself at the head of the men of Northumberland and Cumberland, and lead them, 'and they shall not go in until they either gain their ends, or die in the struggle'. He assured them that he had a plan, but he could not trust the details of it to a letter.[184]

The magistrates in Carlisle swore in some 900 special constables, armed the yeoman cavalry and summoned two troops of dragoons. By the 15th it seems to have been all over. The strike had collapsed, Taylor had failed to appear and the authorities were confident that his influence had evaporated. Yet, within a few days Taylor was active again, assisted by Harney. They led 200 Chartists to disrupt a Sabbath observance meeting, but, although he was staying with James Arthur, other Chartists leaders in the area were apparently distancing themselves from him.

On 23rd August Taylor was in Newcastle, and he gave a lecture in what was called the New Lecture Room. He returned to his call for exclusive dealing, which 'would soon bring the shopkeepers to their senses'. He warned against any precipitate outbreak: 'Let no attempted arrest lead to an outbreak. A few months of imprisonment might be borne, but years would not remedy the slaughter of brothers, and the tears of the widow and orphan'. But he assured them that he would persevere until universal suffrage had been achieved 'even should physical revolution be forced upon them'.[185]

On the following day, O'Connor addressed an open-air meeting in Carlisle and, in the evening, Taylor gave a lecture to a gathering in the local theatre. He talked about a plan 'for working out the great cause', about which he had reputedly consulted William Lovett and John Collins when he was with them in Warwick Gaol. It was, he hinted, a plan that might involve danger. On the other hand, he no longer wanted to be tied by the Convention, but 'to be free and unshackled'. The Convention had sectionalised the movement and was 'in part composed of spies, traitors and cowards'. In a statement which caused a sensation at the meeting, he called for seven men 'who had no fears' in whom the reformers of Cumberland could place confidence, and who would have confidence in him and obey him. Such men would be needed within six weeks and 'they must be prepared to sacrifice all they had before they come to act on the matter. The time for talking was over; the time for action was nearly come'. According to a police witness,

> He said the country was evidently upon the eve of a Revolution and it depended upon the middle classes, whether it could be a bloody one or not, but for his part, he did not care which way it was; it was immaterial to him.[186]

His greatest ire was reserved for the middle classes, who had 'pledged themselves that when they obtained the Reform Bill they would make it a stepping stone for obtaining the freedom of millions', and 'if blood were shed he would blame the middle classes for it.' 'He did not so much blame the aristocracy for keeping aloof from the people, for they were brought up in ignorance of their wants and wishes, but it was different with the middle classes.' Finally, he declared that 'he had always told his constituents he did not believe that moral force would be of any avail against an immoral government' and that their only weapon that had ever brought freedom was 'a good broad sword in their right hand'.[187] He also talked of using force to prevent the convicted Birmingham rioters being transported. The Carlisle magistrates issued a warrant for his apprehension, but by the time they got around to activating it Taylor had headed south again.

On 4th September, back in London, he called for the dissolution of the now much depleted Convention and for the exclusion from any future convention of the existing delegates, who had failed. The implication, according to Lowery, being that somehow the rest of the Convention, whom he had denounced as 'traitors and cowards' had lacked the courage which Taylor and his supporters had.[188] Confronted with this, he declared that a large minority had, indeed, been spies and traitors. Bronterre O'Brien retorted that no one could have much faith in his judgement when he went around declaring his intention to put himself at the head of large body of armed men. O'Connor was against complete dissolution arguing that some guiding body needed to be retained. There had been talk of holding a Provincial Convention and Taylor seems to have accepted that, claiming that he had spoken with various people in London and they were favourable to the idea. He backed the publication of a Declaration of Rights as the closing action of the Convention. It would, according to Taylor, 'show the people, that instead of wishing to destroy the Constitution, the object of the Convention was to go back to their ancient rights and privileges, and establish the Constitution on its original basis'. His proposal was carried against the advice of O'Connor, but the Convention could not agree on a form of words for a final address despite three drafts from Taylor, O'Brien and Peter Bussey. Taylor had criticised O'Brien's earlier draft as 'deficient in vigour and determination'. He told the delegates,

> All constitutional law is at an end; justice is withheld or denied, brute force is now the order of the day with your enemies, the apostate traitors of the Government of Britain. The period has arrived when resistance becomes a duty – submission a crime against God and man; and while it is your duty to see that resistance is effectual in its nature, and as little prolonged as is consistent with your entire success, it is equally ours to place ourselves at the head of our respective constituencies, and taking the post of honour, as it is that of danger, lead them on to the victorious assault of the citadel of corruption, or proudly fall in the breach, another victim of oppression, and another example of undying determination.[189]

Taylor and Bussey then produced a document which according to O'Brien was 'the most thoroughly illegal and dangerous document that issued from any portion of the Chartist body during the whole period of the excitement'. It apparently recommended insurrection. On the final day the few remaining delegates accepted that an address should contain a mixture of all three drafts and Taylor and William Carpenter, another journalist, were given the power to amend it, but, even then, they could not agree, so no final address was issued.[190]

The General Convention of the Industrious Classes finally dissolved on 14 September, a decision carried by the casting vote of the chairman, John Frost from Wales. As the Convention broke up there were a number of meetings between different individuals discussing what ought to happen next. One of these consisted of Frost, Peter Bussey from Yorkshire, W.G. Burns from Dundee and Taylor. Apparently they pledged themselves to work for an armed uprising throughout the country on 3 November. According to William Lovett, Harney, Taylor, Bussey and Cardo had a further meeting at Heckmondwike near Bradford on 30 September and talked of organising a rising simultaneously in the North of England, the West Riding and in South Wales.[191] Taylor, however, denied that he was at that meeting 'where everything was concocted' and said that he was kept in the dark until the last minute about plans devised there.[192]

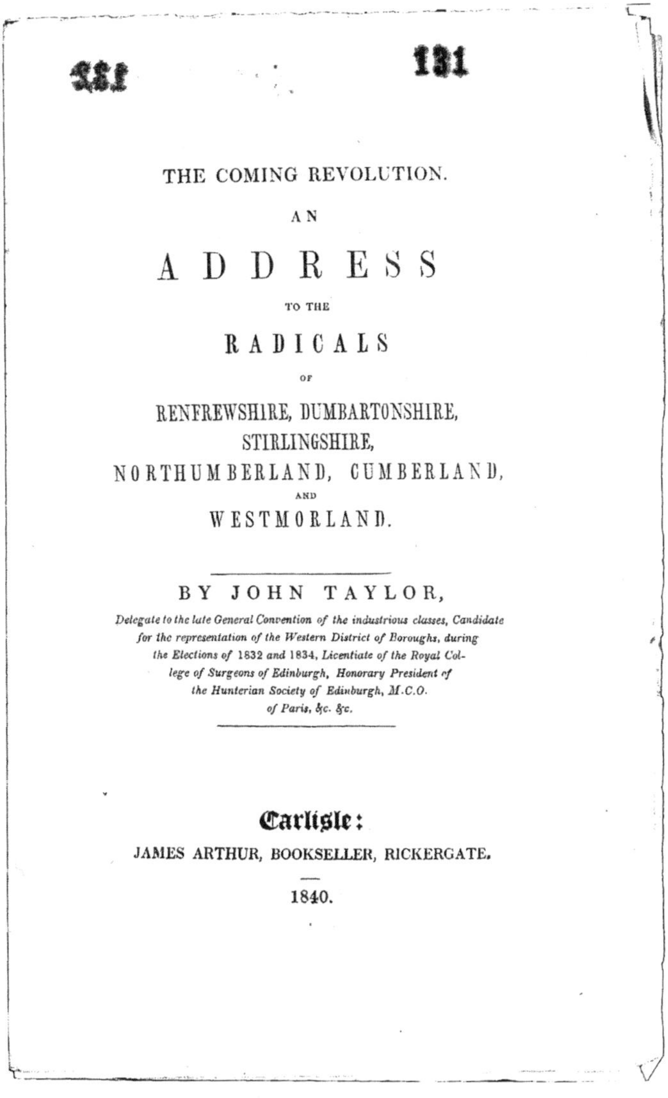

THE COMING REVOLUTION.

AN

A D D R E S S

TO THE

R A D I C A L S

OF

RENFREWSHIRE, DUMBARTONSHIRE,
STIRLINGSHIRE,
NORTHUMBERLAND, CUMBERLAND,
AND
WESTMORLAND.

BY JOHN TAYLOR,

Delegate to the late General Convention of the industrious classes, Candidate for the representation of the Western District of Boroughs, during the Elections of 1832 and 1834, Licentiate of the Royal College of Surgeons of Edinburgh, Honorary President of the Hunterian Society of Edinburgh, M.C.O. of Paris, &c. &c.

Carlisle:

JAMES ARTHUR, BOOKSELLER, RICKERGATE.

1840.

**Illus. 7: Dr John Taylor's pamphlet, *The Coming Revolution.*
(National Archives)**

Meanwhile Taylor was addressing meetings of the Northern Political Union and had presumably been discussing the possibility of armed insurrection with people.[193] General Napier, in charge of the Northern Command of the army, now regarded Taylor as the most violent of the

Chartists, beside whom O'Connor was relatively moderate. Napier believed that Taylor now saw O'Connor as an enemy whom he wanted to push out of the way.[194] Certainly his attacks on O'Connor now became more open. He accused the Council of having paid themselves more money than the Convention had authorised and he accused O'Connor of having used the national rent, to which all associations contributed, as a bribery tool to buy support from specific members of the Council.[195]

Taylor continued to talk about impending revolution, publishing a pamphlet addressed to the Radicals of Renfrewshire, 'Dumbartonshire', Stirlingshire, Northumberland, Cumberland, and Westmorland, entitled *The Coming Revolution*, in which he talked of 'the mighty convulsion … about to shake to their centre all the institutions of the world'. He believed that the financial system was near to collapse and this would lead to disorder. Politicians were interested only in maintaining office, while manufacturers were so busy acquiring and enjoying wealth that they had 'no ear for the cry of the starving mechanics'.

> Rising in desperation, the people will not be content with the mere reform of abuses, but will destroy every remnant of a system under which they have suffered so much, and instead of pausing respectfully at the foot of the throne, may overturn the throne itself.[196]

Yet, despite the supposed plotting for insurrection, Taylor seems to have been remarkably relaxed. He found time during October to begin publication of the History of the Convention in the *Northern Star* and in the *Scottish Patriot*. It combined detailed minutes with remarks on some of the issues that had arisen. In Carlisle the magistrates felt confident enough to ask for the troops to be withdrawn, since the movement had become 'apathetic'.[197] In spite of the language, the authorities took no action against him at this stage, and while they were opening the letters of O'Connor, Lowery, O'Brien, Henry Vincent and many others there was no mention of looking at Taylor's. Lowery complained that Taylor was reckless to be still sending letters about a possible rising through the post.[198]

At the Heckmondwike meeting or soon afterwards, Bussey asked for more time and it was decided to postpone the rising until Christmas Eve. Depending on the version believed, either Frost was not informed of that decision or, in Taylor's belief, the Welsh would not wait. On 4 November came the Newport uprising or riot (depending on one's point of view) in Wales. John Frost and a large contingent of Chartists and miners descended on Newport, were met by troops and twenty or more of the Chartists were killed and more than fifty seriously wounded. It followed weeks of secret manoeuvrings.

According to William Farish, a young handloom weaver and Chartist from Carlisle,

> The rising in South Wales, with the abortive attempt at insurrection by Frost, Williams and Jones, were not the isolated affairs which many supposed. They were certainly well known beforehand in Carlisle, and if successful might have been imitated in a fashion there, but more extensively on the banks of the Tyne and Wear.[199]

The Hammersmith Chartist, Henry Ross, told O'Connor, soon after Newport,

> that Dr Taylor and others were actually selling commissions; that Major Beniowski was to be appointed commander-in-chief, as he was a good officer; and as soon as the battle was fought and won, that then Beniowski, as he was a dangerous and ambitious man, was to be shot.[200]

According to Taylor's own account, on the other hand, on 29 October, the Tuesday before the Newport rising, he was in London and Henry Hetherington called on him after midnight with a stranger who said that he was from Yorkshire, and who informed him of an imminent rising in Wales. He had had no communication with Frost since the dissolution of the Convention. The stranger was apparently Charles Jones, who had been the Convention delegate for Llanidloes and Newtown, and who was in hiding after earlier riots in Llanidloes.[201] Although telling Taylor of the projected rising he 'could give no precise details'. However, Taylor claimed that, in the meantime, and in the presence of Hetherington, he wrote to Frost saying that he has just heard of the plan and that he would be 'found at my post'.[202] Taylor was instructed to head north and he borrowed money and set off at once. In Yorkshire he met with Peter Bussey, where they talked of the possible Yorkshire rising, and they sent a messenger to Wales asking the Welsh to delay the rising for ten days. Taylor then headed for Newcastle and Carlisle. There he found that O'Connor and O'Brien's open hostility to the idea of a general strike or other direct action had left in its wake complete disunity and suspicion. While Taylor was trying to undo this and preparing his people for action, the news of the rising in Wales arrived.

On the other hand, there is some evidence that Taylor knew more than he admitted. Robert Lowery, writing long after, and who was in Dundee at the time of Newport, says that he was approached by W.G. Burns, who had been Forfarshire delegate to the National Convention, who said that Taylor had contacted him to say that a rising in Wales was due to break out immediately. But Lowery had regarded this as no more that a typical piece of 'brag and mystery' by Taylor. There is a further evidence of implication, however, in an intercepted letter from an anonymous lady friend in London on 13 November, which seems to imply that Taylor might have been expected to be 'mixed up in the late dreadfully unfortunate proceedings in Wales'.[*] Various people had visited her house after the rising and 'all express their surprise that your name was not more prominent in the later movement'. She found the failure of the Welsh rising 'most extraordinary and unaccountable' and 'beyond the comprehension' of all in London, 'success seemed so certain'. The explanation could only be that those taking part in it were 'dastardly cowards'. Full of admiration for Taylor, she went on to say that doubtless he would be more successful in the North, having 'gloriously defeated the authorities in Carlisle'. 'Were all leaders like you our cause would be certain,' she flatteringly declared. She was in touch with the émigré Russian-Polish radical, Major Bartholemew Beniowski, delegate for Tower Hamlets, and member of Harney's East London Democratic Association, who was awaiting the call from Taylor to come north to act as commander-in-chief of the Chartist forces.[203] According to another source, Taylor, soon after Newport was writing,

> The Pole has not gone to Wales, but I understand a much honester man. If I were Mrs Frost there should be a Wife of Wales as well as a Maid of Saragossa, and daughters too! What have such dainty dames to do with home? They could at least mount a horse and head a squadron, and I know one lieutenant who would charge through hell to serve them.[204]

Taylor's standing in Newcastle had been undermined by Devyr and the *Northern Liberator*, who defended O'Connor. On the night after the Newport rising, 5th November, but probably before news of it would have reached the North, Taylor was in Newcastle giving what even the critical *Northern Liberator* described as a brilliant address to a packed meeting, although, judging from the police transcript of the speech it seems something of a ramble. Much of it was devoted to an attack on the Mayor, John Fife, paradoxically a fellow surgeon and a man who had been active in the 1831-32 reform campaigns. He also called for a new Convention and, tongue in cheek, and, to the delight of the audience, he announced that he would counsel them 'to be quiet and orderly and wait the time till a merciful providence would make them free'.[205] He reasserted his republicanism.

---

[*]   The full text of the letter is in the Appendix, page 93.

If I was at the Head, the Republic would be declared. All then cease
to pay rents. The property to become their own. All farmers of not
more than 200 acres to become the sole proprietors, and never to be
sold.

He urged his listeners to take as their text, 'he who would be free, must first
strike the blow' and claimed that he would shoot the man who attempted to
execute a warrant for his arrest.[206] He announced that he would return to
Newcastle on the 9th to address them on the science of gunpowder.

When John Frost, William Jones and Zephaniahh Williams were
arrested for their part in Newport, Taylor spoke at meetings to raise a
defence fund for them and hinted at the need to be prepared to defend Frost
and his associates by force. There were even false reports of Taylor being
in Newport some ten days after the rising.[207] He was in Carlisle on the 6th
and went to Wigton and Dalston on the following day. He had hoped to
address a meeting in the assembly room in Carlisle on the 8th, but
permission was withdrawn.[208] There was criticism of the magistrates for
failing to arrest him, and the Tory *Carlisle Patriot* suggested that he had
deliberately come to see if he would be arrested. The magistrates met to
discuss tactics and eventually decided to send an officer to Wigton to try to
arrest him, but they missed him. Taylor now set off for Newcastle and took
an omnibus in Carlisle from the house of the newsagent, James Arthur,
where he was staying, to the railway station on the 7th. The omnibus was
stopped by the police, but Taylor ducked under the seat and was not seen.
He missed the train and went back to Arthur's house, but the police did not
visit the house. He then set off walking to Brampton where he stayed all
night and then caught the 9 am train to Newcastle. He left the train at
Blaydon and walked into Newcastle by way of Redheugh. After a short
time there, he went to Shields but returned to Newcastle for his planned
evening meeting on the 9th. There was some of the usual tone about his
address. Having denounced an aristocracy that paid spies, bribed juries and
had a servile press, he asserted that he would shoot the men who attempted
to execute an arrest warrant against him. Part of the lecture included
information on gunpowder and rockets and, indeed, the lecture may in fact
have been advertised as a chemistry lecture. Whatever the case, he then
reverted to his apocalyptic warnings,

A crash and a crisis was approaching. When he left London all were
looking for the arrival of the Liverpool steamer from America,
expecting nothing but news that all the American banks were
broken. In anticipation of this, the Bank of England had five
millions of one pound notes ready for circulation, and parties had

taken means to have those notes counterfeited … a crash would come during which the Government, he feared, would attempt to do the people harm.[209]

He escaped from the meeting without being arrested after a decoy was decked out in his hat and cloak and carted off to the police station. Taylor then walked to the village of Winlaton where he stayed for a couple of days. Winlaton was an old iron-making village where there was a lot of support for insurrection and which was the main supplier of pikes and other weapons that would be necessary. Early on the morning of the 11th he set off for the lead-mining village of Alston, high in the Pennines, on foot through the Derwent Valley and Allendale, but lost his way and slept in a farmhouse. From Tuesday 12th until Saturday 16th he was in Alston, living under an assumed name, James Harper, staying at a beer shop kept by Jonathon Woodmas. Although an informer said there were only two Chartists in Alston, it was claimed that he had had secret meetings with miners in Alston Moor where he had urged them to arm themselves, 'and be in readiness, as upon a day shortly to be fixed upon when they would be joined by several thousands from the West, then proceeding into Northumberland, and being reinforced with 700 men with rifles from Winlaton, they would take possession of Newcastle'.[210] Interestingly letters arrived for him in Alston, including the one from his lady friend in London, which might seem to indicate that his visit there was part of a plan. His mail was, however, being intercepted by the local postmaster and passed to Lord Howick's agent. Taylor left Alston on the 16th when he heard that information on his presence there had been sent to Carlisle. His aim was to get to Penrith and, from there, to catch the coach to London.[211] A police officer had been sent from Carlisle to arrest him at Alston, but by the time he got there Taylor had gone. He had set off south, wading across the South Tyne, but he was pursued in a gig, provided by Lord Howick's agent, in torrential rain and eventually arrested, after trying to make a bolt for it, at the Cleikum Inn near Melmerby.

> His bushy whiskers were shaved off, and his luxuriant locks shorn of their once-boasted amplitude. His dress was that of one of the lowest class of miners, with a pair of heavy 'high-low' shoes without ties.[212]

Reputedly, he had only three halfpennies in his pocket when he was captured and when he was taken to Carlisle people commented on the marked change in his appearance, much thinner than a few months before. Illness was clearly already taking its toll. He was charged with sedition for his speech of 24 August and brought before the magistrates. The main witness against him was a policeman, Glaister, who, under questioning by Taylor acknowledged that he had not taken notes of Taylor's speech at the meeting itself, but had made the notes afterwards. The editor of the *Carlisle Patriot* made clear that he was very unwilling for his notes to be used as evidence. Taylor was released on bail after the week-end in gaol on bail of £200 from himself and £100 each from two sureties. A Mr Coultard and Mr Hunt came up with the sureties for his release. A large crowd met him outside the police office and escorted him to the 'Andrew Marvell' Tavern.[213]

Illus. 8: The Cleikum Inn, near Melmerby.
(*photo* Hamish Fraser)

It is not clear if it was rage or panic that made him dispatch a rambling letter on 21 November to the Home Secretary, Lord Normanby, whom he claimed to have once met in Tuscany, where Normanby had a villa, and even to have participated in Normanby's favourite pursuit of amateur dramatics there. The letter denounced Normanby as a 'blockhead aristocrat', a philanderer with 'grizettes of easy virtue, and English ladies of ruined reputation' and 'below contempt'. It accused him of having opened Taylor's letters and used spies and bribery to try to incriminate him. He claimed that forged seditious letters were being sent to him from Wales intended to suggest that he was implicated in the uprising there and to entrap him by getting him to respond.[214]

There is no evidence that he attended the secret convention of Northern and Borders' delegates held in Newcastle on 1st December. On Sunday 8 December in Dalston, near Carlisle, presumably at a Chartist Church, he told them 'to be ready as they would be wanted before three weeks'. Dalston was a village with a very lively Chartist group and a local squire who apparently preferred hunting to administering justice. While there, Taylor delivered a lengthy prayer which conjured up a nightmare image of possible impending death and destruction.

> Almighty and everlasting God, thou great first cause, whose word called into existence this beautiful world, whose will sustains it amid the realms of space, and whose fiat can again consign it to the Chaos from which it originally sprung; who has created man in thine own image, endowed him with faculties capable of exquisite enjoyment, and placed him in circumstances where everything in nature should minister to his happiness; with no law to bind him but the law of thy will, easy to be understood and delightful to follow, leading ever to happiness here and eternal bliss here after: O Eternal God of Justice, we pray thee now to look down in compassion upon they creatures, sunk from the high estate to which thou hadst called them, and pining in want and wretchedness through a miserable existence, to which thy loving kindness never destined any one, and to which only the institutions of wicked men in opposition to thy Holy Will and Word have reduced them. Grant us now comfort and hope from above while we engage in services of grateful devotion to thee: Be present with us according to thy promise that whenever two or three are gathered together in thy Name there thou will be in the midst of them, to bless them and to do them good. Overrule our words to the end that we may speak that wisdom which is not in us, and which cometh only from above, and so dispose us to speak and hear as it becomes the oracles of the Living God to be spoken and to be heard.

> Teach us Great Lord that the great object of life is to learn how to depart from this scene of our earthly pilgrimage with a Patriot's hope and a Christian's confidence, and so to act in every varying scene of this transitory world, that we may neither be ashamed to live nor afraid to die, and as we shall wish we had done when that hour draws near.

> Ruler of Earth and Heaven, if it be thy will let the cup of thy wrath be turned away from this unfortunate Nation: Soften the hearts and enlighten the understandings of our cruel and obdurate rulers, so

that peace and comfort may once more gladden the homes of thy creatures, and time be given to them to know and appreciate thy goodness, and worship thee in Spirit and in Truth amid the songs of joyful thanksgiving for all the blessings thy liberal hand has so bountifully scattered around.

Nevertheless, O Lord, not as we will but as thou wilt; if the iniquities of our rulers are not yet full, and that the nation's guilt for having so long submitted to them requires a heavier punishment; if want and misery with death on the pale horse are to stalk triumphant through the land; if desolation is to reign over our beautiful fields, and the groans of dying mothers and the shrieks of famishing children, to be the only requiem over their murdered husbands and fathers, brothers and friends, till like a second Jerusalem all is horror: grant us patience to endure and courage to resist: enable us to meet adversity with firmness, and prosperity, if such be thy will, with calmness, so that our lives, if preserved, may be useful to our fellow creatures, or if lost in the struggle, that our deaths may be honourable to ourselves, advantageous to the Nation and acceptable to Thee.

We commend to thy fatherly care the widows and orphans wherever they are, or whom we may be obliged to part from in defence of our Freedom, that noblest boon that thou has bestowed upon us. Our prayers are offered up not for a sect but for mankind, wherever thou has planted a human family we desire to look on them as brothers, and confident in the honesty of our intentions and the justness of our cause, we appeal to thee our only judge, through Jesus Christ our only Saviour.

AMEN.

The prayer was reissued as a card and widely distributed. It is the first inkling of what was to be an increasingly Christian fervour from Taylor. Although the Scottish Chartist movement in particular had a strong Christian Chartist element within it, Taylor had never been part of this and, indeed, the Christian Chartists had generally seen him as a dangerous, physical-force advocate hostile to their gentler philosophy of spiritual regeneration.

That same day, he wrote a letter to Mary Ann Groves, who had been secretary of the Female Political Union, in Birmingham. It revealed that he still thought insurrection a possibility.

Frost shall not be tried, or will have companions he little thinks of, keep this in mind and be astonished at nothing, depend upon it there

will be a merry Christmas, all here are preparing for a national
illumination, I presume in anticipation of the Queen's Marriage but
you know best: these Radicals are terrible fellows, at least half a
dozen Emissaries have been sent to see what state the North of
England was in and the universal feeling is that there is no country
like (illegible), this is partly to be attributed to the vast extent of
Moorland which has generated a race of hardy Poachers all well
armed, and who would think themselves disgraced if they missed a
moorcock flying seventy yards off: this together with the number of
Weavers necessarily in want has made a population ripe for action
and its Neighbourhood to the Scottish border, with the facilities for a
guerrilla warfare, are said to have (illegible) to make it the
Headquarters for a winter campaign.

His continuing disenchantment with O'Connor was also apparent.

It is said your Irish Friend O'Connor, has proved himself the coward
his enemies always called him, having before betrayed the men of
England in the matter of strikes has now refused to take part with the
men of his own county, (Yorkshire) – he is agitating for money to
pay lawyers, as if money could save Frost when he knows that every
lawyer would give ten years Briefs to hang him, if it is to be done at
all, other means must be used and the Chartists are not worth the
name of men if they don't try them.[215]

On 10 December he was at a meeting of delegates in Manchester, called to
discuss plans for action to save John Frost and his companions, whose trial
was scheduled for the end of the month. There he seems to have been
hinting at possible links between Chartists and French republicans, with two
of the French agents reputedly staying with him at some point. General
Napier was pretty sceptical about a real link. If it did exist, he suggested,
then it 'must be a trial between the leaders which can cheat the other, and it
will die when they discover that neither have cash'. As he said, if the
French were plotting rebellion against their monarchy they were not going
to have funds to help British Chartists. Perhaps this was no more than
Taylor playing on his supposed earlier experiences as a revolutionary in
Paris. Napier noted in his diary for 12 December:

Dr Taylor told the meeting to be ready with their arms; that he had
seen two revolutions, one in Greece and one in France, and he hoped
to see one in England. This was received with loud cheers and cries
of we are ready. He said he did not wish them to injure others, but
their neighbours were rolling in plenty and he supposed those he

addressed were too fond of their wives and children to let them starve, and that they would *dust their oppressors' coats well*.[216]

According to a police informer, James Harrison, he was informed by John Hodgson that

> Dr Taylor had volunteered either to stay at home amongst his own men in Carlisle district, or he would come into Yorkshire to head and assist them, or he would go to Wales. We consider him the best man we know. He said that Dr Taylor had 900 men ready to rise well armed and well fit up in every respect and that he had bought 1000 shirts for his men at 2/6 each, with 2 pockets for ammunition at the breast and a belt for pistols or sword. He also said it was determined that Taylor should stay at home.[217]

Taylor himself later wrote of approaches from various people reporting on impending planned risings in Yorkshire and Lancashire, but he suggests that he was very suspicious of these and decided to wait until people had actually taken to the field. On 19 December ten delegates, including Beniowski, met at a convention in London, and according to O'Connor, reports of what Taylor was reputedly planning were, apparently, received 'with disgust'.[218]

In spite of his statements, which were certainly seditious, it was not until 21 December that a warrant was issued by the Home Secretary to open all of Taylor's mail in Carlisle and to get rid of letters unless a way would be found to explain the delay in delivery. The warrant stayed in force until June 1840,[219] but, once again, it seems odd that the authorities had been so slow to act since the mail of many others had been regularly opened for months.

In Newcastle and Yorkshire, groups of activists now awaited the signal for an uprising to begin, timed to coincide with the sentencing of Frost and his companions. The date scheduled was 12 January. But, on the day before, O'Connor's *Northern Star* came out firmly in support of only constitutional action to save Frost and his associates from the gallows. A few took to the streets in Dewsbury with muskets. In Sheffield another few attacked the police after their leader, Samuel Holberry, had been arrested. In Newcastle a handful of activists awaited the summons to arms and, when none came, fled. Of Taylor there was no sign, and the account of events in Newcastle by Thomas Devyr makes no mention of him. Meanwhile in Yorkshire, his associate from Edinburgh, Robert Peddie, was intriguing with Peter Bussey and others over a January rising in Bradford and other West Riding towns. It was betrayed by a police informer and the leaders arrested on 27 January. Disastrous as these risings were for many of the participants, they do seem to have persuaded the authorities to commute the death sentences on Frost and his associates to transportation for life.[220]

How far Taylor was carried away by his always fertile romantic imagination and how far it was the demon drink to which he was succumbing is far from clear. There is a wildness in his language, as if he were courting arrest. At the same time, he seems to be recoiling from the prospect of what might be unleashed. It may be that he had a sense of impending death. After all he was a doctor and must have been aware that with tuberculosis, the likely cause of his ill-health, his time was short. That and drink gave a frantic edge to some of his activities. There is no doubt that physically and mentally Taylor was in decline. In an intercepted letter to John Wilkinson in Newcastle, at the beginning of January 1840, he claimed that he had 'no secrets and was connected with no secret societies' and that he knew nothing of Peddie's activities, although Peddie had been in Carlisle at around this time.[221] In the circumstances, he felt that decisions had to 'be left to the opinions of the different localities, to act as they think best under their own separate leaders'. It is only at a later stage, 'when some mighty convulsion has taken place that one leader may be required to guide the mass'. He also expressed frustration that lawyers were preventing his getting access to his private funds to carry out his schemes.[222] The Carlisle magistrate's clerk was again complaining that 'those villainous Chartists are all alive with us', but that it was impossible to get information because 'none but the initiated get into their meetings'.[223]

According to O'Connor, around the time of the rising in Bradford on 26 January, Taylor told him of his plan to organise the seizure of Newcastle, Carlisle, Durham and Edinburgh. He asked O'Connor,

> If he thought he could sufficiently trust Lowery to put him in possession of the town (Newcastle) and barracks, he was then going to Carlisle to put James Arthur in possession of that town and barracks. He asked Arthur to recommend him a man to put in possession of Durham Castle, and he would put John Duncan in command of the town and castle of Edinburgh.

He also claimed that he had purchased a ship in Ayr, *The Black Joke*, 'and selected a crew of men, who had been with him in Greece, and who belonged to a Republican Association'. These would intercept the vessel in which Frost and his colleagues were to be transported and bring them back to Ayr.[224] One can only assume that this was either fantasy or irony. O'Connor's response to his wild talk was, 'I always thought you mad, but

I'm sure of it now'. Taylor then, true to form, borrowed £10 from O'Connor to take him home.[225]

Just how extensive the Northern conspiracy was and how far Taylor was at the centre will probably never be entirely clear. In 1873 David Urquhart, a former diplomat who for nearly forty years had been convinced, and was determined to convince others, that the threat to world peace and to British interests came from Russia, added his view. He constantly argued that Russia was involved in nefarious conspiracies against the British Empire, conspiracies that could include even the Foreign Secretary, Lord Palmerston. He saw the Chartist risings of 1839 as one of these Russian-inspired conspiracies. According to Urquhart, Taylor 'a vain and shallow man' was in cahoots with Beniowski, who, according to Urquhart was 'the contriver and director of the whole plot' and in the employ of the Russian secret service. Beniowski was the leader of a group of five – William Cardo, who was a staunch advocate of Urquhart's ideas in the 1840s, John Warden, Westropp and an unnamed individual 'who at that time held a high position in the police'. According to this account, Urquhart, discovering this Russian conspiracy, managed to stop it everywhere except Newport. He claims to have met Taylor at the time and, in a five hour meeting, argued the case against Chartism and insurrection. Taylor reputedly asserted, 'I don't care about convulsion. I believe convulsion to be the only remedy for our evils and I desire that others should be as reckless as myself'.[226] The true facts behind Urquhart's statements are equally difficult to unearth.

The exact timing of Taylor's meeting with Urquhart is not clear. It may have been in August or September 1839, after the collapse of the then strike plans, and when Urquhart was visiting various parts of the country. Alternatively, it may have been in early 1840 when Taylor was clearly going through some kind of physical and mental crisis. Urquhart's account of the meeting, however, does give some sense of Taylor's state of mind at the time.

> I never so shook any man. He seemed tortured, struggling between responsibility, shame and failure brought home, and self-love and pride that linked him to a system, and the greater shame of sinking in the estimation of those he had led on. … I must add that Dr T. repeatedly asserted that bloodshed and convulsion were inevitable. The die was cast.

Taylor gave Urquhart some letters of introduction to people who might help him, but noted, 'I believe we have parted never to meet again'.[227] On the other hand, he may have been influenced by Urquhart's arguments to the extent of beginning to doubt the tactics he had been advocating. Also, if

Mary Ann Groves is his unknown lady friend, then there is probably significance in the fact that she became an enthusiast for Urquhart's cause.[228]

Certainly if Taylor was at the centre of a real conspiracy he was the most inept of conspirators. His speeches are full of promises of armed rebellion. His pamphlet on *The Coming Revolution* was circulated with its scheme of rebellion. He was still writing open letters with promises of commitment to be at the forefront. The fact that he remained at liberty perhaps indicates that the authorities had ceased to take him seriously.

Chapter Seven:

'Gifted with talents of a very high order'

Dublin, Published by James M'Glashan, 1851.

Illus. 9: Drawing of John Taylor from *Christian Lyrics*.
(Carnegie Library, Ayr)

In early January 1840 a new Chartist paper *The Regenerator and Chartist Circular* was launched in Manchester by T.P. Carlile. The tone of some of the writing in the first issue is very much that of Taylor, with a letter signed by 'A Radical' declaring that there was no hope from the middle classes and denouncing those 'sham radical traitors; who would persuade the producers of all wealth that the middle classes were their friends'. Even if it was not he who wrote the piece he was certainly in touch with the editor and the issue included an inspirational poem by him, 'To the Memory of Augustus Hardin Beaumont, Esq.':[229]

Beaumont! Thy name shall last
Amid the patriot few,
Who nailed their colours to the mast
When lowering clouds the sky o'ercast
In danger, tried and true.

The Islands of the West
Where there your days were spent,
Shall number thee amid the blest,
The Champion of the race oppress'd,
On Justice sternly bent.

Should Belgium strike again
For freedom as of yore
She'll think upon the God-like men
Who cheered her on to victory then,
And who are now no more.

And Spain's red fields shall be
Another altar still,
Where men shall learn to act like thee,
And in the hearts of brave and free
Thy hallowed name shall thrill.

Then of the soul sincere,
The free and dauntless heart,
Scotland forgets thee not, her tear
Was shed o'er thy untimely bier,
In grief from thee to part.

England reveres thee yet,
Who taught her sons their power;
Time shall not teach her to forget
The proud example thou hast set
In danger's darkest hour.

Live in the minstrel's song,
Live in the poet's lays;
Live! for thy deeds to worlds belong,
Protest the right, resist the wrong,

Live in undying praise.

So when the battle's near,
And gathering hosts are nigh
Thy name to every freeman dear,
Shall nerve his hand, his heart shall cheer
Till on the bloody field the conquered tyrants lie.

On 3 February, Taylor and O'Connor were in Manchester meeting with local Chartists to set up a meeting of Chartist delegates to devise some way of procuring a free pardon for Frost and his colleagues. According to the Mayor, there was 'a sort of feeling that something is to take place'. There seems to have been quite a deal of tension in the ranks as to how best to proceed and Taylor was reported to have set off for Liverpool.[230] However he was back for the meeting of delegates in Manchester and he took on the role of secretary to the meeting. In his brief contribution to discussion he declared that the people of Cumberland were prepared to do anything, 'but were all of the opinion that any violence would be most injurious'.[231] A few days later he addressed a meeting of the Carlisle Radical Association on the Sands at Carlisle, the Mayor having refused them permission to meet in the Market Place. It was a bitterly cold day, with snow falling at intervals and a very ill Taylor was brought from his sick bed, wrapped in rugs, to address the meeting, but, after speaking for a few moments, he was too ill to continue.[232]

The planned prosecution against him was dropped, perhaps because of his physical condition, although the recently-appointed Whig mayor of Carlisle, told Lord John Russell that the magistrates did not feel that there was enough evidence to convict him. Also, Taylor had threatened to cause embarrassment by cross questioning the Whig magistrates on their speeches during the 1832 Reform campaign.[233] When O'Connor saw him again in York some weeks later in early March he was shocked by his appearance. He was not able to stand alone (either from drink or illness) and had to be assisted by a Chartist friend from Hull. According to O'Connor the conversation went,

O'Connor: 'Good God, Taylor, what's the matter!'
Taylor: 'Why, my heart is broken.'
O'Connor: How? Have you been at your old tricks?'
Taylor: 'No, no – damn it – that would never kill me; but that villain has murdered me.'

The 'villain' was William Ashton, a Barnsley Chartist, who in a letter just printed in the *Northern Star*, was accusing people of having betrayed Frost and conspired against O'Connor. Part of the letter read,

> Murder will out, but the time has not yet come. I cannot, however, refrain from slightly alluding to one of those gentlemen who cut a conspicuous figure at the late Manchester delegate meeting. My God! The effrontery of this fellow surpasses anything I could have imagined. Does he suppose there are none in England to bear witness against him, and his accomplices? Does he imagine that the memorial to her Majesty with 20,000 signatures has been overlooked? Does he forget his promise and his childish and criminal (not carnal) dalliance with Mary Ann for five weeks? If he do, let him think of THE RESULT, and take his caution and retire from advocating a cause which has received much injury from his base treachery. If he take this advice he may maintain his character; if not, he shall hear from me in plainer terms.

Taylor took it as a reference to himself, telling O'Connor that he 'couldn't care what the villain wrote or said of me, but to make poor Mary Ann – as innocent and virtuous a girl as ever lived – the victim of his malice was damnable'.[234]

One can only assume that the comment by O'Connor to Taylor having been 'at his old tricks' is a reference to Taylor's drinking. Reputedly, he was drunk later that day and damning O'Connor and the *Northern Star*. And Mary Ann? We can only guess. Alas, little is known of the details of the women activists in the movement, of whom there were undoubtedly many. The name Mary Ann appears to have been remarkably common among them. The most likely possibility is Mary Ann Groves, the secretary of the Women's Radical and Female Political Union in Birmingham, who became a warm supporter of the Urquhart cause.[235] But there was Mary Ann Grocock of Westminster, whose letters were being opened at the end of 1839 after she had received one from someone in Alston.[236] Might it even be Mary Ann Walker, a London Chartist? Intriguingly in the week that Taylor died Mary Ann Walker was giving a talk on the terrible conditions of some women workers in High Holburn. She was dressed in mourning. It was assumed in the report that it was because of the death of her father some months before. Who's to say that it was not for poor Taylor?

After March 1840 Taylor largely disappears from view. He was to have been a material witness at O'Connor's trial at York but was too ill to appear. O'Connor said that he spent about a month in Carlisle with James

Arthur, holding meetings denouncing O'Connor, but this may have been in February. Soon afterwards he was in Hull, where his old associate W.G. Burns was now based, and said that he was going to the continent for health reasons.

Out of the blue, in May 1841, he wrote to William Lovett (whom he addressed as 'My Old Friend') in London from St. Catherine's, Carrickfergus, in the north of Ireland, having seen some of the attacks on Lovett in the pages of the *Northern Star*. His letter contained a bitter assault on O'Connor as 'the worthless and false-hearted demagogue' and concluded,

> Nothing is worth fighting for but a Republic, it will never be got but by fighting, and that so long as O'Connor possesses any influence, the people will never be allowed to fight with any chance of success, for that or any other object, however they may be hounded or partial outbreaks by inflammatory speeches in a paper like the Star which blows hot and cold in the same column, and that in short the man who according to his own account was to die in the last ditch for the defence of Freedom, would not stir across the gutter to obtain it if there were a chance of even wetting his feet. Holding these opinion I say I have long ceased to interest myself in what is going on in the political world being content to know that however abused at present I shall not be less welcome when my services are required if an opening for exertion should occur in my day, and when disappointment shall have opened the eyes of the masses to the quandary of which they are frequently the victims.[237]

He declared that he no longer involved himself in political matters 'where I saw no prospect of being able to effect any good and had no longer either fortune or health to throw away in the cause'. But he also seemed to imply that he might yet have a role. He believed that O'Connor was trying to pack the council of the Charter Association with his own nominees, two of whom at least were 'the most unblushing scoundrels in England'. He clearly still had fears of arrest since he asked Lovett to divulge his address to no one. Lovett replied and asked Taylor to give his account of what he knew about the Newport uprising. Taylor provided some information and self-justification, returning an eight page account in different letters to different addresses, lest any of them was opened by the authorities. He still believed that attempts were being made to entrap him by means of letters from unknown correspondents asking for information.

In July 1841 his old enemy Peter Mackenzie is commenting that 'he is scarcely now so much as heard of'.[238] A piece by him headed 'Taxation,

Misgovernment, Means of Redress' was published in *McDouall's Chartist and Republican Journal* in July 1841, but it was an old article first published in the *True Scotsman*. It returned to the familiar theme of boycotting tea, tobacco and alcohol.

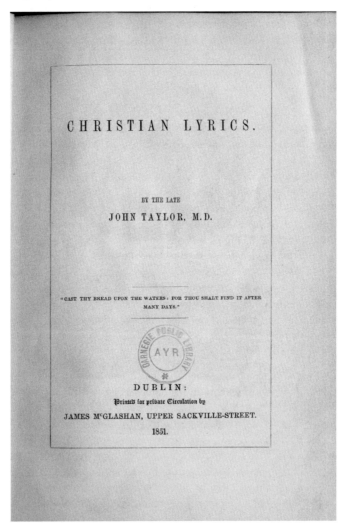

Illus 10: *Christian Lyrics.*
(Carnegie Library, Ayr)

According to Hovell, even by early 1840, Taylor 'was hurrying himself by his excesses to his grave'.[239]   However, he lingered for nearly two years, dying in Larne, on 4 December 1842 at the home of his sister and brother-in-law, Rev James Smith, the Church of Ireland rector of Islandmagee. During his last months he wrote a number of poems, most with a religious flavour and sixteen of these were published privately in 1851 as *Christian Lyrics*, for the benefit of the Archdeacon's Provident Fund, his brother-in-law having become Archdeacon of Connor.   The quality of many of the poems is high, but the tone is melancholy, contemplating death and eternity. In *Where is our Home?* he asks where is the home of the sailor, the soldier, the lover, the student, and the merchant and reminds them that the concerns of this world pass. Only in the lines on the merchant is there some echoes of his radical past, the merchant who dreams of 'his wealth untold' from the mines of Ophir, bought with blood and 'cursed with the Negro's echoing cries'.

> And well for the merchant could he have known
> To make wealth a passport to Glory's throne;
> Had he cloth'd the naked, and fed the poor,
> To the houseless wand'rer had ope'd his store
> Had he sought the couch of sorrow and pain,
> To win them to health and joy again, –
> He would not now, at his utmost need,
> Have lamented his trust in a broken reed;
> No cry of the slave would his hopes destroy,
> No tear of the orphan would check his joy,
> But paeans glad from a thousand throats
> Would utter his advent with glorious notes!

In lines to a young friend who had just died there is something of the same.

> The rich, the proud, they pass
> From earth's glad scene away,
> Like shadows o'er a glass,
> Or stars before the day.
> They leave no trace of tears
> Upon a pallid cheek,
> And memory for one short week;
> The soulless marbles tell their tales,
> But none their early death bewails.

In a number of the poems there is a sense of life that has gone leaving little 'But misfortune's sighs, or affliction's tears', but, at the same time a hope that it may 'leave some mark that in after years / May awhile defy oblivion's powers'.

Among the poems is one, to an unnamed person, a lament for a lost love,

> There is a flower, whose modest eye
> Is turned with looks of light and love
> Who breathes her softest, sweetest sigh
> Whene'er the sun shines bright above.
>
> Let clouds obscure, or darkness veil,
> Her fond idolatry is fled,
> Her sighs no more their sweets exhale, –
> Her loving sigh is cold and dead.
>
> Canst thou not trace a moral here,
> False flatterers of the prosp'rous hour?
> Let but an adverse cloud appear,
> And thou art faithless as the flow'r.

In others, the romanticism of Byron and Shelley is appropriated, as it was by so many Chartist poets in these decades,

> The rushing tempest, and the roaring sea,
> The fiery lightening darting through the sphere,
> The thundering voice, that others trembling hear,
> Have charms for me.

But there is little sign of its being given the distinctive Chartist bite, which Miles Taylor has detected in the poems of Ernest Jones.[240]

The *Northern Star* made no mention of his death, but the *Ayr Advertiser* was remarkably generous, remembering him fondly.

> We think we see him yet on the platform! – his full black eye kindled with his subject and his long dark hair in graceful curls on his shoulders. On such occasions, fluent in speech, felicitous in expression, and impassioned in delivery, the tones of his rich and melodious voice fell like bold music on the ear, while his nicely balanced sentences never failed to elicit a shudder at this deadly-aimed sarcasm, a burst of applause at the fervour of his appeals to the patriotic feelings, or a hearty laugh at his many depictions of the ludicrous.[241]

And he continued to be remembered in Ayr. In October 1844 a group of Ayr Chartists met at the Ayr Arms Inn to celebrate his birth and to remember Taylor's 'unceasing efforts for the diffusion of civil and religious liberty'. His businessman uncle, George Taylor, 'although differing in opinion from the large company assembled', joined in the occasion.[242] Presumably, it was soon after this that the decision was made to collect money for a monument to Taylor. Public meetings were held and a committee of management appointed and £25 collected.[243] The original idea was to erect a monument in Ayr or in Alloway Churchyard, but, after much to-ing and fro-ing the Churchyard directors refused consent on the grounds that it was a place only for burials. The committee met with similar refusals from elsewhere. Eventually a spot was found at Kingcase Old Church, near Prestwick, between Ayr and Kilmarnock. But this was objected to by the Ayr people who argued that the money collected ought to be spent in Ayr.

The memorial plan hung fire for a number of years. However, a letter in the press at the end of 1856 solicited the information that the committee, consisting of old Chartists like John McWhinnie and Alexander Smith,[244] was still in existence and that a memorial in the form of an obelisk on a Corinthian column was planned at the cost of £70. The committee was hopeful of raising the additional money 'from the wealthy of Ayr', who had not yet been tapped for support.[245] The revival of interest may have come from talks about memorials for O'Connor who had died in 1855. There were plans afoot for memorials to him in Nottingham, London and Edinburgh. There was also, as *The Times* noted, something of a 'monument mania' in the 1850s and this was accompanied by contestation over who and what should be commemorated.[246] Working-class radicals were keen to have their heroes remembered. The opportunity of a site came with the opening of a new cemetery on the edge of the old-established and distinct working-class community of Wallacetown on the north side of the river from Ayr. At some point the decision was made to go for a statue, and James Shanks, a Glasgow sculptor, was commissioned to produce it.[247] There was still some difficulty in raising the necessary money – now £80 – and a concert in September 1858 incurred a loss of £4. None the less, the project went ahead. Those who remembered him seemed to think that the statue was a fair likeness, which might indicate that a portrait of him existed. As it is, we have only one line drawing of him in his last months. The Masonic ceremony avoided any reference to his political activities and even the dinner in the evening concentrated on his good works: 'he was perhaps too zealous, but take him all in all, he was an earnest, honest man … [and] as a medical man the poor never needed to apply to him in vain'.[248] None the less, the raising of the statue is perhaps an indication of how quickly the physical-force aspects of Chartism were being forgotten and of how rapidly 'moderate' Chartist demands and language were being incorporated into Scottish Liberalism.

There was nothing very original in the content of Taylor's speeches. The sentiments were those of a fairly traditional radical, harping back to old rights, accusing the government of subverting the constitution. Even as the Convention was dissolving, he was arguing that its object had been the restoration of the ancient Constitution and the history of the Convention on which he embarked gives no sense that he saw it as a revolutionary alternative to Parliament. But this was the discourse of popular radicalism at this time. As James Epstein has argued, much radical debate was still rooted in the eighteenth-century arguments about the English constitution which claimed historical antecedents for English democracy in pre-Norman times. As he says, 'there was often little sense of incompatibility between the traditions of popular constitutionalism,' which emphasised historical precedent, 'and those of Paineite republicanism', which did not look back, but argued for a new, written, democratic constitution.[249] Taylor was able to move back and forth between the two discourses. Although critical of the middle class for failing to come into the Chartist movement, there is rarely any critique of the developing capitalist system. Getting the vote was the right of all citizens, but there were few suggestions of what might be done with the vote. In spite of his industrial background, with family money much involved in coal and chemicals in Ayrshire, it is as a landed and professional man that Taylor presents himself.

The flamboyance and the rhetoric both fit an image of the romantic hero. Again and again he conjures up a picture of his leading an uprising, sabre in hand. There were frequent assertions that he was prepared to die for the cause. In practice, of course, it never got beyond fiery rhetoric. One wonders if this was the reason for his sudden collapse and disappearance from the movement early in 1840. He had been among the foremost in talking of uprisings. Judging from the intercepted letter from his lady friend in London great things were expected of him at the end of 1839 and yet he did little. Was it guilt at his failure to live up to his own image of the romantic hero that was the reason for the 'tortured' figure 'struggling between responsibility, shame and failure brought home, and self-love and pride' that David Urquhart saw? Did he perhaps think that the excitement of the platform had led him to statements and claims in which he did not really believe?

Perhaps, of course, it was no more than intimations of mortality that explain his sudden departure from the movement. There is no doubt that drink and tuberculosis – and perhaps laudanum – were taking their toll on his health, which had never been very good. As a medical man, he would have been aware – as he hinted on more than one occasion – that his days were limited. Certainly, the fervent embracing of the Christian faith at about the same time, evident in the Dalston prayer and then in the *Christian Lyrics* he was composing over his months of illness do seem to indicate a soul anxious about eternity. On the other hand, perhaps, like so many others, it was political disillusionment that drove him away. He had undoubtedly lost faith in O'Connor and he found it increasingly difficult to work with someone who seemed inconsistent and ready to undermine agreed tactics. In contrast, he had come to admire the integrity and quieter tactics of William Lovett.

In the end, we can only guess at his emotions and his thinking from the relatively meagre sources available. His contribution to the early Chartist movement, however, had been an important one. He had been one of the earliest to denounce the Whig 'betrayal' after 1832 and to take up the case for the working-class vote. He saw Chartism as part of a wider international movement for democracy. He was one of a number of flamboyant figures who helped create a national movement for the People's Charter, linking the Scottish movement with activities in England. Despite the delicacy of his health, he travelled up and down the country making speeches and there is a consensus that his speeches were inspiring. Oratory played a vital part in creating the Chartist movement and all were agreed that in Taylor's speeches there was 'the happiest combination of natural gifts and artistic power'. Of course, like many of the Chartist speakers, he adjusted his speeches to his audience, often sounding more militant in places where a call to arms would raise a cheer than in those parts where it was better to press his plans for exclusive dealing. Harney complained that some Chartists had 'one set of speeches for the North and another set of speeches for the metropolis' and Taylor was operating in Newcastle and Cumberland where the rhetoric, but perhaps not the reality, was expected to be revolutionary. Even Robert Lowery had to succumb to the expectations of his audience, and he defended it 'as a form of democratic control involving the rank and file of the movement in a complex mutual relationship of expectation, performance and response'.[250] But that was a necessary tactic for those involved with the mass platform agitation. And the fervour was always there. Although the language in the speeches is often that of arming and threatening change by force, in practice his most consistent argument is that for an economic boycott, as he urged through his Dhurna societies. He came back to this again and again. But what he clearly came to believe was that the cause could not be won without the threat of force, hence his constant assertion that people had the right to retain arms.

Despite all his vanities, his foibles and his failures, like many an eloquent drunkard, he was able to charm those with whom he had contact and was able to retain their loyalty. Even his critic, Robert Lowery, who believed that 'Vanity was his ruling passion' admitted to his generosity:

> He would share his last sixpence with anyone, and freely offer the
> loan of any he had at the time to those whom he knew to have none;
> so often of that which he defrauded others he could give the greater
> part away.[251]

But, it was not just charm that made him attractive to his loyal supporters. Clearly there was a recognition in Ayrshire that in his brief but eventful life he had made real sacrifices for the radical cause in which he believed.

**Illus. 11: Drawing of 'Island Magee' Church from *Christian Lyrics*.
(Carnegie Library, Ayr)**

Appendix

Letter to Taylor from an anonymous lady friend in London, enclosed in letter from John Grey, Dilston to Lord Howick, 20 November 1839 in Papers of 3rd Earl Grey, Durham University Library, GRE/B102/7/4,5

London 13 November 1839
Dearest,

Letter relieved all here from dreadful state of suspense. Silence appeared unaccountable – searched newspapers in vain for news from the North – doubtless intercepted by Government – expected to see your name mixed up with late dreadfully unfortunate proceedings in Wales. The failure there is most extraordinary and unaccountable – it is beyond the comprehension of all here, success seemed so certain – you surely must have heard of the dreadful defeat of the Chartists in Wales. – you do not mention it yet it involves so much. I expected you to have cleared up this mysterious and unaccountable affair – you I am sure will manage better. It has shown the absence of a good general there. You have gloriously defeated the authorities in Carlisle – were all leaders like you our cause would be certain. OB is particularly anxious to know your movements.

The Pole is particularly anxious to know when his services will be required. I know his address but dare not send it by letter. I have received two letters. One from Lord Stanhope with three copies of Morning Herald wherein is a copy of the Resolutions.

Our house has been besieged by persons enquiring for you. – and they all express their surprise that your name was not more prominently forward in the late movement. A meetings was held at Merthyr – several speakers – did not hear their names – they said they would seize two aristocrats for every Chartist leader sustaining any injury. Surprised and confused and confounded at the late disastrous and cowardly affair. – So great a body of men to be defeated by a mere handful of soldiers – cause sustained a great defeat by such dastardly cowards.

Yours devotedly,

Endnotes

Chapter One: 'Every inch a gentleman'

[1]   *Ayr Advertiser*, 21 October 1858.

[2]   John Taylor, *Christian Lyrics*, (Dublin, 1851).

[3]   Paul A. Pickering and Alex Tyrrell, *Contested Sites: Commemoration, Memorial and Popular Politics in Nineteenth Century Britain* (Aldershot, 2004).

[4]   Edward Royle, *Chartism* (London, 1996), p. 25; James A. Epstein, *Radical Expression: Political Language, Ritual and Symbol in England, 1790-1850* (Oxford, 1994), p. 19.

[5]   Alexander Wilson, 'John Taylor, Esq. M.D. of Blackhouse, Ayrshire (1805-1842)', *Ayrshire Collections*, Vol. 1 1947-9 (AANHS, 1950).

[6]   Patrick Joyce, *Visions of the People: Industrial England and the question of class, 1848-1914* (Cambridge, 1991), pp. 39-40; John Belchem and James Epstein, 'The Nineteenth century gentleman leader revisited', *Social History*, 22 (2), May 1997, pp. 174-193.

[7]   For other examples see Owen R. Ashton and Paul A Pickering, *Friends of the People: Uneasy radicals in the age of the Chartists* (London, 2002).

Chapter Two: 'Eyebrow dark and eye of fire'

[8]   *Air Advertiser*, 19 September 1805.

[9]   A biographical note in the *Glasgow Liberator* in the 1830s gave his date of birth as 5 October 1805: see *The Operative* 17 March 1839.

[10] Alexander Wilson suggests that it was his mother who was Indian and this may have been believed by some of Taylor's fellow Chartists. See, for example, Brian Harrison and Patricia Hollis (eds), *Robert Lowery: Radical and Chartist* (London, 1979), p. 118. Annabella's brother, William, named the industrial village he established in 1802 near Dalmellington, Patna, presumably from his mother's home area.

[11] A.J.G. Cummings, 'Industry and Investment in the Eighteenth century Highlands: The York Buildings Company of London', in *Industry, Business and Society in Scotland since 1700,* A.J.G. Cummings and T. M. Devine, eds., (Edinburgh, 1994), pp. 24-42.

[12] National Library of Scotland (NLS), Yule 116(2). Petition and complaint of John Taylor, Esq of Blackhouse, William Taylor, Esq. of Nethermains, George Taylor, Merchant in Ayr, Sons and General Disponees of the deceased John Taylor, Writer to the Signet, 17 February 1812.

[13] C.A. Whatley, 'The Process of Industrialisation in Ayrshire, c. 1707-1871', unpublished Ph.D., University of Strathclyde, 1975.

[14] The Diploma of the Royal College of Surgeons of Edinburgh, which in 1815 became the Licentiateship, was initially a means of examining country surgeons but was later used as a cheaper method of acquiring a basic

medical qualification for those who could not afford to go to Edinburgh University. I am grateful to Steven Kerry of the RCSE for this information.

[15] It may be that the estate was already sequestered by the creditors as early as 1816.

[16] This was well short of the initial valuation of over £57,000 and it took a long time to find a buyer. See *Air Advertiser*, 15 November 1827 and 3 April 1828 for announcement of judicial sales to try to get rid of the estate.

[17] National Archives of Scotland (NAS) CS96/4543 Scheme of division among the creditors of the deceased John Taylor, Esq of Blackhouse at Martinmas 1829.

[18] *The Operative*, 17 March 1839. Only a single copy of *The Liberator* seems to have survived, but the profile of him was republished in Bronterre O'Brien's paper *The Operative* with which Taylor was associated.

[19] L.C. Wright in *Scottish Chartism* (Edinburgh, 1953), p. 219 suggests that this was during the aftermath of the assassination of the Duc du Berri, but that was in 1820 when Taylor was only 15.

[20] *Northern Star* 16 March 1839. This is a report of a speech by Taylor and it refers to La Petre as one of the hospitals, but I take this to be a mishearing of La Salpêtrière. It was a hospital intended for the poorest.

[21] A.B. Spitzer, *The French Generation of 1820* (Princeton, N.J., 1987), p. 67.

[22] A.B. Spitzer, *Old Hatreds and Young Hopes The French Carbonari against the Bourbon Restoration* (Cambridge, Mass, 1971), p.222.

[23] Jill Harsin, *Barricades The War of the Streets in Revolutionary Paris, 1830-1848* (Basingstoke, 2002), p.p. 13-17.

[24] *Northern Star*, 16 March 1839.

[25] Peter L. Thorslev, Jr., *The Byronic Hero: Types and Prototypes* (Minneapolis, 1962), pp. 66-8.

[26] *Northern Star*, 15 June 1839.

[27] Thomas Frost, *Forty Years' Recollections: Literary and Political* (London, 1880), p. 102 suggests this and says that he was given 48 hours notice to leave the country.

[28] The last part of Beer's account is equally doubtful. Augustus and Arthur Beaumont were in France in 1830-31 and again in 1834. If Taylor was there in 1830 it was very briefly. W. E. Adams, *Memoirs of a Social Atom* (London, 1903), Vol. I, p. 211 also had the story.

[29] *Carlisle Journal*, 28 December 1838.

[30] *Newcastle Weekly Chronicle*, 5 January 1889.

Chapter Three: 'An extremely clever but wayward young man'

[31] For McDouall and Schofield see Ashton and Pickering, *Friends of the People*.

[32] *Air Advertiser,* 13 October 1831.

[33] *Ayr Observer,* 14 August 1832; *Air Advertiser*, 16 August 1832.

[34] *Air Advertiser*, 15 October 1832; *Ayr Observer*, 2 October 1832. Taylor was unhappy with the report in the *Observer* of his speech at the Kennedy meeting and sent a long letter outlining the contents. Much to his

[35] indignation, the *Observer* cut part of the letter. *Ayr Observer*, 16 October 1832.

[35] *Air Advertiser*, 18 December 1832.

[36] *Glasgow Journal and Evening Post*, 22 December 1832.

[37] *Ayr Observer*, 25 December 1832. This includes the polling lists with the names of those who voted for the different candidates. Wilson wrongly says he had only 131 votes.

[38] It was noticed in the *Scots Times*, 16 June 1832. The evidence for Taylor having been involved in it comes from his biographical details published in *The Operative* in 1839.

[39] James Paterson, *Autobiographical Reminiscences* (1871) plays down the author's radical background in the 1830s.

[40] *Case of Duel and Statement of the Conduct of T.F. Kennedy, Esq. of Dunure, M.P., One of the Lords of His Majesty's Treasury, Member of the Society for the Diffusion of Useful Knowledge, &c, &c towards one of his opponents at the last election for the Ayr District of Burghs by John Taylor*. Kilmarnock: Printed for the Author at the Ayrshire Radical Press, by J. Paterson, (1833). This pamphlet is the source of the above account of the proceedings. *Reformers' Gazette*, CLXXIII, 27 August 1836.

[41] NAS, CS 46/157 T.F. Kennedy v. John Taylor, James Paterson, Robert Nelson and Alexander Hutchison, 18 March 1833.

[42] It was still being published in June 1833 when it reported a meeting in Cumnock calling for the dismissal of government ministers. Taylor was probably at that meeting. See *Weekly True Sun*, 16 June 1833.

[43] *The Operative*, 17 March 1839.

[44] *Air Advertiser*, 17 October 1833; *Ayr Observer*, 15 October, 22 October, 17 December 1833.

[45] *Air Advertiser*, 31 October 1833.

[46] James Paterson, *Autobiographical Reminiscences* (1871), p. 114.

[47] *Air Advertiser*, 16 January 1834.

[48] James Howie, *An Historical Account of the Town of Ayr for the last Fifty Years* (Kilmarnock, 1891), pp. 101-103.

[49] *Air Advertiser*, 22 January 1835; *Glasgow Evening Post and Paisley and Renfrewshire Reformer*, 24 January 1835.

[50] *Air Advertiser*, 18 June 1835.

[51] Whatley, 'Industrialisation in Ayrshire', pp. 196-208.

[52] *Air Advertiser*, 13 March 1834.

[53] *Ibid.*, 4 February 1836.

Chapter 4: 'A lava-like eloquence that set on fire all combustible matter in his path'

[54] Other descriptions are in R. C. Gammage, *History of the Chartist Movement* (London, 1894, reprinted 1969), pp. 28-9.

[55] J.D. Burn, *The Autobiography of a BeggarBoy* (London, 1855), p. 128.

[56] Owen Ashton, 'Orators and Oratory in the Chartist Movement', in O. Ashton, R. Fyson and S. Roberts, eds., *The Chartist Legacy* (Rendlesham, 1999), p. 54.

57   *Glasgow Argus*, 30 October 1834.
58   *Glasgow Evening Post*, 7 May 1836.
59   *Glasgow Argus*, 5 May 1836.
60   *Ibid.*, 25 July 1836.
61   *Reformers' Gazette*, CLXXIII, 27 August 1836.
62   *Glasgow Journal and Evening Post*, 20 October 1836.
63   British Library, Place Papers, Add. Ms 35,150.
64   *Glasgow Argus*, 15 June 1837 quoted in Montgomery, 'Glasgow and the Movement for Corn Law Repeal', *History,* 64 (1979) p. 367.
65   Beaumont (1798-1838), born in New York and brought up in Jamaica, with his brother Arthur has all the ingredients of the romantic hero, both having been involved in revolutionary activities in Brussels and Paris in the early 1830s. See W. H. Maehl, 'Augustus Hardin Beaumont: Anglo-American Radical', *International Review of Social History*, XIV (1969), pp. 237-50.
66   Archibald Prentice, *History of the Anti-Corn Law League* (1853.   This edition Cass, 1968), p. 49.
67   *Scottish Patriot*, 23 November 1839.
68   W.E. Adams, *Memoirs of a Social Atom*, p. 211.
69   Gammage, *History*, p. 29.
70   Harrison and Hollis, *Robert Lowery*, p. 118.
71   *Glasgow Argus*, 8 December 1836.
72   *Scotsman*, 17 December 1836.
73   *New Moral World*, 1 July 1837 quoting *The Liberator*.
74   *New Moral World*, no. 140, 1 July 1837 quoting *The Liberator*.
75   For Monteith, see B. Aspinwall, 'The Scottish Dimension: Robert Monteith and the Origins of Modern British Catholic Social Thought', *Downside Review*, January 1979.
76   J.D. Burn, *Autobiography*, p. 132.   Burn's account confuses the by-election in May 1837 with the general election in July; *The Operative*, 17 March 1839; *Scotsman*, 26 July 1837.
77   *Reformers' Gazette*, CXC, 29 July 1837.
78   The full song can be found in the Glasgow Broadsides and Ballads on the web at http://special.lib.gla.ac.uk/teach/ballads/index.html
79   *The Operative*, 17 March 1839.
80   John Fraser's *True Scotsman* was still advertising this pamphlet, *Letters on the Ballot* by John Taylor, Editor of the Glasgow *Liberator*, in April 1839.
81   Copies of *The Liberator* do not survive covering the period of the strike, but these comments were in the *New Liberator*, 6 January 1838.
82   For the background to the strike, see W. Hamish Fraser, 'The Glasgow Cotton Spinners, 1837' in *Scottish Themes*, edited by John Butt and J.T. Ward (Edinburgh 1976).
83   *Glasgow Evening Post*, 28 October 1837;   *Northern Liberator*, 4 November 1837.
84   *Monthly Liberator*, No III, 9 June 1838.
85   *Northern Liberator*, 2 December 1837.

[86] Dorothy Thompson, *The Chartists: Popular Politics in the Industrial Revolution* (Aldershot, 1986), p. 6.

[87] James Epstein, *The Lion of Freedom: Feargus O'Connor and the Chartist Movement, 1832-1842* (1982), p. 50.

[88] *Glasgow Argus*, 18 December 1837. Elections at least every three years had been abandoned in 1716 in favour of ones only every seven years.

[89] *Glasgow Argus*, 1 January 1838; *New Liberator*, 6 January 1838.

[90] *Glasgow Argus*, 1 January 1838.

[91] W. H. Maehl, 'Augustus Hardin Beaumont', pp. 237ff.

[92] Mark Hovell, *The Chartist Movement* (1918, 1966 reprint), p. 91; *Northern Star*, 6, 13 January 1838.

[93] Joan Hugman, 'A Small Drop of Ink: Tyneside Chartism and the *Northern Liberator*' in *The Chartist Legacy,* Owen Ashton, Robert Fyson, Stephen Roberts, eds., (Rendlesham, 1999). Within a month, in January 1838, Beaumont was dead. By the end of 1837 Upper Canada was in open rebellion, led by William Lyon Mackenzie, against the unelected governing councils.

[94] *New Liberator*, 6 January 1838.

[95] *Ibid.*; *Glasgow Argus*, 8 January 1838

[96] *Ibid.*

[97] *Scotsman*, 10 January 1838; *Reformers' Gazette*, CXCVI, 3 February 1838.

[98] *Northern Liberator*, 13 January 1838.

[99] Henry Jephson, *The Platform: Its Rise and Progress* (London, 1892), quoting an account in the Place Papers.

[100] *Ibid.*

[101] W. Lovett, *the Life and Struggles of William Lovett, in his pursuit of Bread, Knowledge and Freedom* (London 1876), p. 158-9.

[102] *Glasgow Chronicle*, 14 February 1838.

[103] *Glasgow Saturday Post*, 7 April 1838.

[104] *Glasgow Chronicle*, 28 May 1838.

[105] J.T. Ward, *Chartism*, (1973), p. 95.

[106] *Monthly Liberator*, III, 9 June 1838.

[107] *Northern Star*, 18 August 1838.

[108] *Glasgow Saturday Post*, 23 June 1838.

[109] Harrison and Hollis, *Robert Lowery*, p. 118.

[110] *Northern Star*, 3 May 1845.

[111] *Ibid.*, 28 July 1838.

[112] *Glasgow Saturday Post*, 14 July 1838.

[113] The *Northern Star*, 2 July 1838 names John Cowie, Charles Matheson, John Cumming, Robert Rogers and Peter McDonald, none of whom had featured prominently in earlier campaigns.

[114] *Northern Star*, 7 July 1838.

[115] *Ibid.*, 23 June 1838.

Chapter Five: 'To strike down the tyrant who tramples down the rights of the poor'

[116] *Northern Star*, 27 October, 17 November 1838. Craig was born in Dunlop in 1795 and trained as a draper with Swan & Edgar in London before setting up in business on his own in Kilmarnock in 1818. He took an active part in the Reform campaign of 1831-32 and was elected to the town council. He pulled out of the Convention in July 1839. He died in 1858.

[117] *True Scotsman*, 17 November, 22 December 1838; 19 January 1839; *Northern Star*, 22 December 1838.

[118] R. Lowery, *Address to the Fathers and Mothers, Sons and Daughters, of the Working Classes, on the system of Exclusive Dealing and the formation of Joint Stock Provision Companies, shewing how the People may Free themselves from oppression* (Newcastle upon Tyne, 1839).

[119] *True Scotsman*, 17 November 1838'; *McDouall's Chartist and Republican Journal*, No 14, 3 July 1841.

[120] *True Scotsman, Northern Star*, 22 December 1838. The other members of the committee were Taylor, president, Hector Grant, vice-president, Joseph Spedding, secretary; John Nelson, vice-secretary, Samuel Irvine and Daniel Cumming; *Glasgow Courier*, 17 December 1838.

[121] *Glasgow Chronicle*, 17 December 1838.

[122] *Northern Star*, 15 December 1838. The resolution was moved by Burns from Dundee and Fyfe from Crieff.

[123] Articles on Aberdeen Chartist leaders by William Lindsay are in *Aberdeen People's Journal* 19, 26 February 1887.

[124] Patrick Brewster, *Chartist and Socialist Sermons. With an introduction by Thomas Johnston* (Glasgow n.d.), p. 86; see also *The Operative*, No 7, 16 December 1838.

[125] Patrick Brewster, *Chartist and Socialist Sermons*, p. 23: Chartist Sermon II, 'The Snare of Armed Revolt'.

[126] *Northern Liberator*, 27 October 1838 quoted in W.H. Maehl, Jr, 'The Dynamics of Violence in Chartism: A Case Study in Northeastern England', *Albion*, vol 7 (2) (1975), p. 107.

[127] Harrison and Hollis, *Robert Lowery*, p. 118. Green was the traditional radical colour.

[128] *True Scotsman*, 26 January 1839.

[129] *Carlisle Journal*, 28 December 1838; *True Scotsman*, 12 January 1839.

[130] *Northern Liberator*, 5 January 1839. The letter was from an unidentified member of the Northern Political Union.

[131] *True Scotsman*, 26 January 1839; *Northern Liberator*, 19 January 1839; Joan Hugman, ' "A Small Drop of Ink" ', p. 38.

[132] Interestingly, Harney was to marry a remarkable Ayrshire woman, Mary Cameron, the daughter of a weaver in Mauchline. She was active politically alongside her husband, but unfortunately died at a relatively young age. The marriage is reported in the *Ayr Advertiser*, 24 September 1840.

[133] Harrison and Hollis, *Robert Lowery*, p. 118.

[134] *Northern Liberator*, 2 February 1839.

[135] *Ibid.*, 26 January, 1839.

[136] *True Scotsman*, 12 January 1839.

[137] *Ibid.*, 26 January 1839. Alva and Tillicoultry had objected to the selection of Alexander Halley, who was associated with Fraser and the Calton Hill people, as the delegate for Stirlingshire and were determined to put up a candidate more representative of their views.

[138] Brian Harrison, 'Chartism, Liberalism and the Life of Robert Lowery', *English Historical Review*, Vol. 82, 1967, p. 508.

[139] *The Operative*, 10, 17, 24 March 1839; Gammage, *History*, p. 107.

[140] *Air Advertiser*, 21 February 1839; Birmingham Central Library, Lovett Collection, LF76.13.

[141] *Northern Star*, 6 April 1839. O'Brien was absent at the end of February and in early March after the tragic death of a young daughter whose clothes caught fire.

[142] *Ibid.*, 16 March 1839.

[143] *Ibid.*, 30 March 1839.

[144] Birmingham Central Library, Lovett Collection, LF76.13.

[145] R.J. Richardson, *The Right of Englishmen to have Arms ... as shown in a speech delivered to the National Convention ... in 9th April 1839*, quoted in James A. Epstein, *Radical Expression: Political Language, Ritual and Symbol in England, 1790-1850* (Oxford, 1994), p. 3.

[146] Epstein, *Radical Expression*, p. 12; Miles Taylor, 'The Six Points: Chartism and the Reform of Parliament' in *The Chartist Legacy*, edited by O. Ashton, R. Fyson & S. Roberts (Rendlesham, 1999), p. 5.

[147] *True Scotsman*, No 28, 27 April 1839.

[148] *Northern Star*, 6 April 1839; *True Scotsman*, 4 May 1839.

[149] British Library, Place Papers, Add. Ms 34,245, Taylor to the Chairman of the Convention, 3 April 1839.

[150] *Reformers' Gazette*, 4 May 1839.

[151] A. Wilson, *The Chartist Movement in Scotland*, p. 75.

[152] *Weekly True Sun*, 12 May 1839.

[153] Hovell, p. 153; *Northern Liberator*, 25 May 1839.

[154] *Northern Liberator*, 25 May 1839.

[155] *Carlisle Journal, Carlisle Patriot*, 25 May 1839.

[156] *Northern Star*, 1 June 1839.

[157] *True Scotsman*, 15 June 1839.

[158] Harrison and Hollis, *Robert Lowery*, p. 137.

[159] It is not clear if there was any Chartist influence in this, but it is perhaps significant that one of the local shoemakers, John McPherson, the one non-weaver charged, fled.

[160] NAS AD 14/39/433 Fox Maule to the Lord Advocate 21 May 1839

[161] *Ibid.*, Provost of Forfar to the Solicitor General. 28 May 1839.

[162] *Ibid.*, Solicitor General to Lord Robert Kerr, 13 June 1839.

[163] *Dundee Courier*, 18 June 1839, quoted in Shona Gail Paul, 'Dundee Radical Politics 1834-1850', M.Phil Dundee University, 1999, p. 69. Burns's true

views are difficult to pin down, since at the Convention he also spoke against the address drafted by Bronterre O'Brien which hinted at arming and at preparation to resist oppression. Hovell, *Chartist Movement*, p. 147; Lovett, *Life and Struggles*, p. 205.

[164] *Northern Star*, 29 June, 6 July 1839.

[165] Gammage, *History*, p. 124; *Northern Star*, 6 July 1839.

[166] *Ayr Advertiser*, 11 July 1839; *Northern Star*, 6 July 1839.

[167] *Weekly True Sun*, 7 July 1839; James Epstein, *The Lion of Freedom: Feargus O'Connor and the Chartist Movement, 1832-1842* (1982), p. 170.

[168] *Weekly True Sun*, 7 July 1839.

[169] Perhaps William Hawkes Smith a noted socialist and phrenologist. Seventeen people, including Taylor, were arraigned before Warwick Assizes on 2 August. All pleaded not guilty. Five were brought to trial and the others, including Taylor, were sent back. Three were condemned to death. *Northern Star*, 10 August 1839.

[170] *Scottish Patriot*, 13 July 1839.

[171] National Archives, Kew, (NA). HO40/53/75.

[172] Lovett, *Life and Struggles*, p. 218-21.

[173] Gammage, *History*, p. 133.

[174] A copy of the handbill is in the Peel Correspondence in British Library, Add Mss 40, 427 F.74; see also *Carlisle Journal*, 13 July 1839; Thomas Ainge Devyr, *The Odd Book of the Nineteenth Century* (New York, 1882), p. 180.

[175] NAS GD45/9/32 S.M. Phillips to Mayor of Newcastle, 22 July 1839.

[176] D.J. Rowe, 'Some aspects of Chartism on Tyneside', p. 30.

[177] *Northern Star*, 3 August 1839, cited in Dorothy Thompson, *The Early Chartists*, p. 197.

[178] The Forth was a meeting space in the area that is now Newcastle Central Station.

[179] D.J. Rowe, 'Some Aspects of Chartism on Tyneside', p. 30; Devyr, *The Odd Book of the Nineteenth Century*, p. 177.

[180] *Scottish Patriot*, No.3, 20 July 1939.

[181] Attwood got caught up in his favourite topic of paper currency and Lord John Russell was able to point out that the Convention had come out firmly against it.

[182] Epstein, *Lion of Freedom*, p. 172.

Chapter Six: 'One of the most dangerous characters in the movement'

[183] *Reformers' Gazette*, CCXV, 31 August 1839.

[184] Tyne and Wear Archives, John Brown Papers 1666/2/1, James Willoughby to John Brown, 13 August 1839.

[185] *Northern Liberator*, 31 August 1839.

[186] NA, HO40/54/149.

[187] NA, HO40/54/159ff.; *Carlistle Patriot*, 31 August 1839.

[188] Harrison and Hollis, *Robert Lowery*, p. 142; NA HO. 40/54/149 Letter from the town clerk of Carlisle, 29 January 1840, reporting an address by Taylor on 24 August 1839.

[189] *Scottish Patriot*, 28 September 1839.

[190] *Northern Liberator*, 14 September 1839; *Northern Star*, 21 September 1839; 28 June 1845.

[191] Lovett, *Life and Struggles*, pp. 338-41.

[192] Birmingham Central Library, MS 753, Lovett Papers. Taylor to Lovett, 10 June 1841.

[193] Epstein, *Lion of Freedom*, p. 203.

[194] Napier to the Duke of Portland 9 September 1839 in W. Napier, *The Life and Opinions of Sir Charles Napier, GCB* (London, 1857), p.p. 88-9.

[195] *Northern Star*, 21 September 1839.

[196] NA, HO 40.54/131.

[197] June C.F. Barnes, 'Popular Protest and Radical Politics: Carlisle 1790-1850', unpublished Ph.D., University of Lancaster, 1981, p. 344.

[198] Harrison and Hollis, *Robert Lowery*, p. 155.

[199] *The Autobiography of William Farish: The Struggles of a Handloom Weaver* (Private Circulation, 1889), p. 40.

[200] *Northern Star*, 3 May 1845.

[201] David Williams, 'Chartism in Wales', in Asa Briggs, ed., *Chartist Studies* (1965), p. 236.

[202] Apparently since the letter arrived on the day of the Welsh outbreak Mrs Frost immediately destroyed it.

[203] University of Durham Library, Earl Grey Papers, GRE/B/102/7/5, enclosure in letter from John Grey, Dilston to Lord Howick, 20 November 1839. The full text is in the Appendix, page 93. The letter is signed with initials which are impossible to decipher.

[204] 'Chartism; a Historical Retrospect', *Diplomatic Review*, Volume 20, July 1873, p.224.

[205] *Northern Liberator*, 8 November 1839.

[206] Tyne and Wear Archives, John Brown Papers, 1666/7/1; *Northern Star*, 16 November 1839.

[207] Hovell, *Chartist Movement*, p. 184.

[208] *Carlisle Patriot*, 9 November 1839.

[209] *Northern Star*, 16 November 1839; *Scottish Patriot*, 23 November 1839.

[210] *Carlisle Journal*, 30 November 1839, quoting *Newcastle Chronicle*; Tyne and Wear Archives, John Brown Papers, 1666/2/11.

[211] *Carlisle Patriot*, 23 November 1839.

[212] University of Durham Library, Earl Grey Papers, GRE/B102/7/6. John Grey, Dilston to Lord Howick, 18 November 1839.

[213] *True Scotsman*, 30 November 1839.

[214] *Times,* 10 December 1839.

[215] David Urquhart, *Chartist Correspondence*, pp. 3-4 quoted in Epstein, *Lion of Freedom*, pp. 203-4.

[216] Napier, *Life and Opinions of General Sir Charles Napier*, p.98 – 101.

[217] Report from James Harrison, 17 December 1839 in the Harewood Papers, quoted in Dorothy Thompson, *The Early Chartists* (1971), p. 281.

[218] *Northern Star*, 3 May 1845.

[219] NA HO79/4/ 237-8 Private and Secret Entry Books.
[220] Edward Royle, *Revolutionary Britannia?* (Manchester, 2000), pp. 110-112.
[221] Farish, *Autobiography*, p. 37.
[222] NA, HO40/54/123ff.
[223] Tyne and Wear Archives, John Brown Papers, Henry Willoughby to John Brown, 15 January 1840.
[224] *Northern Star*, 3 May 1845. Duncan was secretary of the Edinburgh Chartists.
[225] The problem with the O'Connor account is the timing. The Bradford rising was on 26 January and, at this date, the death sentences still hung over Frost, Williams and Jones. It was not until 1 February that the sentences were commuted to transportation. It was probably in Manchester at the beginning of February that Taylor and O'Connor had their discussion.
[226] *Diplomatic Review*, Vol 20, January 1873, 'Mr Urquhart puts an End to the Chartist Conspiracy'; July 1873, 'Chartism: A Historical Retrospect'.
[227] Gertrude Robinson, *David Urquhart: Some Chapters in the Life of a Victorian Knight-Errant of Justice and Liberty* (Oxford, 1920), p. 101. No source is given for Taylor's account of the meeting.
[228] *ibid*, p. 100.

Chapter Seven: 'Gifted with talents of a very high order'

[229] NA, HO40/45/533, *The Regenerator and Chartist Circular*, No 1, 4 January 1840. Beaumont had been brought up in the West Indies and had been involved supporting the Belgians in their independence struggle in 1830.
[230] NA, HO40/54/595-615, Letters from Charles Shaw to S.M. Phillips, 4, 5, 6 February. 1840.
[231] *Northern Star*, 8 February 1840.
[232] *Ibid*, 15 February 1840; Farish, *Autobiography*, p. 39.
[233] NA, HO 40/45/171; *Carlisle Journal*, 15 February 1840.
[234] *Northern Star*, 29 February 1840; 3 May 1845.
[235] Robinson, *David Urquhart*, p. 100.
[236] NA 79/4, Private and Secret Entry Books, 19 November 1839.
[237] Birmingham Central Library, LF76.13/ 208, Papers of William Lovett.
[238] *Reformers' Gazette*, CCXXXVII, 3 July 1841.
[239] Hovell, p. 187.
[240] Miles Taylor, *Ernest Jones: Chartism and the Romance of Politics 1819-1869* (Oxford, 2003).
[241] Quoted in *Glasgow Saturday Post*, 10 December 1842.
[242] *Ayr Advertiser*, 17 October 1844.
[243] Perhaps £2000 in today's money.
[244] The Committee of Management listed on the back of the pedestal are William Watson, Robert Muir (probably of the Wheatsheaf Inn), William Clark, Alexander Smith (a mason from Wallacetown), John McWhinnie, James Jones (a tea dealer), David Wason and James Murray (a tailor and clothier). The Kilmarnock committee consisted of James Milroy, John Kerry and Daniel Fraser.
[245] *Ayr Advertiser*, 25 December 1856, 8 January 1857.

[246] Paul Pickering & Alex Tyrrell, *Contested Sites: Commemoration, Memorial and Popular Politics in Nineteenth Century Britain* (Aldershot, 2004).

[247] Probably James Shanks (1825/6-1864). See Ray McKenzie, *Sculpture in Glasgow: An Illustrated Handbook* (Glasgow, 1999), p. 115.

[248] *Ibid.*, 21 October 1858.

[249] Epstein, *Radical Expression*, p.11.

[250] Paul Pickering, 'Class without Words: Symbolic Communication in the Chartist Movement', *Past and Present*, August 1976, pp. 150-51.

[251] Harrison and Hollis, *Robert Lowery*, p. 118.

Index

AANHS Publications

Publications of the Ayrshire Archaeological & Natural History Society are available from Ronald W. Brash MA, Publications Distribution Manager, 10 Robsland Avenue, Ayr KA7 2RW.

32	Ayr and the Charter of William the Lion 1205 (Barrow) 20 pages	£1.00
31	Tattie Howkers: Irish Potato Workers in Ayrshire (Holmes) 192 pages	£4.50
30	The Early Transatlantic Trade of Ayr 1640-1730 (Barclay & Graham) 104 pp.	£4.50
29	Vernacular Building in Ayrshire (Hume) 80 pages	£4.50
28	Historic Prestwick and its surroundings, 64 pages	£2.50
27	Ayrshire in the Age of Improvement (McClure) 192 pages	£6.00
26	Servants in Ayrshire 1750–1914 (Aitchison) 144 pages	£5.00
25	The Street Names of Ayr (Close) 128 pages	£5.00
24	Historic Alloway, Village and Countryside: A Guide for Visitors	£2.00
23	The Last Miller: The Cornmills of Ayrshire (Wilson)	£3.00
22	The Rise and Fall of Mining Communities in Central Ayrshire (Wark)	£1.00
21	A Community Rent Asunder: The Newmilns Laceweavers Strike of 1897 (Mair)	£2.00
20	Historic Ayr: A Guide for Visitors, 2nd ed.	£2.50
19	Robert Reid Cunninghame of Seabank House (Graham)	£1.00
18	Cessnock: An Ayrshire Estate in the Age of Improvement (Mair)	£2.00
	Antiquities of Ayrshire (Grose, ed. Strawhorn) (reprint)	£2.00
	Mauchline Memories of Robert Burns (ed. Strawhorn) (reprint)	£2.00
17	John Smith of Dalry, Part 2: Archæology & Natural History (ed. Reid)	£2.00
16	John Smith of Dalry, Part 1: Geology (ed. Reid)	£2.00
15	The Port of Ayr 1727–1780 (Graham)	£2.00
14	Smuggling and the Ayrshire Economic Boom (Cullen)	£2.00
13	Tolls and Tacksmen (McClure)	£1.50
12	The Cumnock Pottery (Quail)	£2.00
11	Robert Adam in Ayrshire (Sanderson)	£1.50
10	The Barony of Alloway (Hendry)	£1.50
9	Plant Life in Ayrshire (Kirkwood/Foulds)	£1.50
6	A Scottish Renaissance Household (MacKenzie)	£1.00
	Armstrong's Maps of Ayrshire (1775: reprint, 6 sheets)	£12.00